ESPORTS IN HIGHER EDUCATION

ESPORTS IN HIGHER EDUCATION

Fostering Successful Student-Athletes and Successful Programs

George S. McClellan, Ryan S. Arnett, and Charles M. Hueber

NEW YORK AND LONDON

First published 2020 by Stylus Publishing, LLC.

First Edition, 2020

Published 2023 by Routledge
605 Third Avenue, New York, NY 10017
4 Park Square, Milton Park, Abingdon, Oxon OX14 4RN

*Routledge is an imprint of the Taylor & Francis Group,
an informa business*

Copyright © 2020 Taylor & Francis Group.

All rights reserved. No part of this book may be reprinted or reproduced or utilised in any form or by any electronic, mechanical, or other means, now known or hereafter invented, including photocopying and recording, or in any information storage or retrieval system, without permission in writing from the publishers.

Notice:
Product or corporate names may be trademarks or registered trademarks, and are used only for identification and explanation without intent to infringe.

Library of Congress Cataloging-in-Publication Data

Names: McClellan, George S., author. | Arnett, Ryan S., author. | Hueber, Charles M., author.
Title: Esports in higher education : fostering successful student-athletes and successful programs / George S. McClellan, Ryan S. Arnett, and Charles M. Hueber.
Description: First edition. | Sterling, Virginia: Stylus Publishing, 2020. | Includes bibliographical references and index.
Identifiers: LCCN 2020026078 | ISBN 9781642671452 (paperback) | ISBN 9781642671445 (hardcover)
Subjects: LCSH: eSports (Contests) | College sports. Classification: LCC GV1469.34.E86 M44 2020 | DDC 796.04/3--dc23
LC record available at https://lccn.loc.gov/2020026078

ISBN 13: 978-1-64267-144-5 (hbk)
ISBN 13: 978-1-64267-145-2 (pbk)
ISBN 13: 978-1-00-344460-2 (ebk)

DOI: 10.4324/9781003444602

This work, like all our work, is dedicated to the students, particularly the students involved in curricular or cocurricular esports programs. Thank you for allowing us to be a part of your lives.

CONTENTS

PREFACE ix

ACKNOWLEDGMENTS xi

1 AN OVERVIEW OF ESPORTS IN HIGHER EDUCATION
What Is It, How Big Is It, and How Does It Work? 1

2 CREATING A SUCCESSFUL ESPORTS PROGRAM
ON CAMPUS 28

3 RUNNING A COCURRICULAR ESPORTS PROGRAM 51

    APPENDIX 3A 66
    Schreiner University Gamer's Guild Creed

4 EXPERIENCES OF AN ESPORTS STUDENT-ATHLETE 72

5 ETHICAL, LEGAL, AND GOVERNANCE CONSIDERATIONS
FOR ESPORTS PROGRAMS ON CAMPUS 86

6 SUMMING UP AND LOOKING FORWARD 113

    GLOSSARY 127

    ADDITIONAL RESOURCES 131

    REFERENCES 133

    ABOUT THE AUTHORS 145

    INDEX 147

PREFACE

Would you be interested to hear more if we told you there was an exciting new program opportunity in higher education that is a huge draw with students, presents a substantial opportunity to raise the profile of an institution and help with student recruitment, is a strong draw for donor and sponsor support, can provide opportunities for men and women equally, and offers a chance to reshape campus culture in ways that recenter academic endeavors on campus? Alternatively, what would you say if we shared that there was an element of college sports competition that posed significant challenges to notions of amateurism; is flush with unregulated and unmonitored cash and recruiting deals; includes significant elements of homophobia, misogyny, racism, and gratuitous graphic violence in its culture; and has been going largely ungoverned? And what if both of these two things are one and the same? We are, and they are. Welcome to esports in higher education.

We want to be clear at the outset. The three of us believe that the intersection of esports and higher education has a lot to offer students and institutions alike. Toward that end, we hope that our work will provide helpful and useful information on how campuses can foster successful esports student-athletes and programs, goals that will not occur as a matter of happenstance. Like any other program or policy implementation, careful and critical thought drawing on the collective knowledge and insights from across the campus community and beyond will be an essential element of any such success story.

Although we are sanguine about esports in higher education, we also believe there are important and serious questions which must be addressed by students, institutions, and governing entities in order to protect student-athletes, colleges, and universities and to ensure important notions of ethics and governance. Those questions and, where we have them, suggestions for addressing them will be shared in this book as well. We urge all involved to begin work in addressing these questions quickly while there is still time to shape esports programs in higher education in ways which are aligned with our core values as educators and which meet our ethical and legal obligations to students and other important constituencies.

Chapter 1 provides an overview of esports and of the ways in which esports is being embraced by college students and by institutions of higher education. Chapter 2 offers advice and insights for colleges and universities that are considering beginning esports programs on their campuses, and chapter 3 addresses the day-to-day management of successful campus cocurricular esports programs. We turn our attention to the experiences of esports student-athletes in chapter 4. Some of the ethical and legal concerns associated with esports are described in chapter 5 before the book moves to its conclusion in chapter 6, which offers a summary of important themes and recommendations from the previous chapters as well as a look ahead to what might be next in esports and higher education. Readers will find a glossary of terms and a list of resources in the book as well.

A note about nomenclature and spelling; We have chosen to follow the guidance of the Associated Press in using *esports* throughout the book where we are responsible for the choice of words and spelling. Astute readers will note other spellings for the term appearing in quoted material as the convention regard to generally accepted form has not been settled. We also use *esports* as singular in form.

Legal issues are discussed at various points throughout the book. We enter these discussions as informed practitioner-scholars (and, for one of us, as an attorney). However, nothing shared in our work is intended as legal advice. We encourage readers to consult with counsel early and often for such advice.

There may be a few folks who have picked this book up (or have had it shared with them) who know little, if anything at all, about esports but are curious about the topic. Other readers have heard of esports, are aware that it is big among students and starting to be an increasing organized presence on campuses, and are here to learn more about what esports is and how esports might fit into higher education. Others of you reading this know a fair amount about esports and picked up this book to learn about how you and your institution might move forward with considering, implementing, or maintaining esports programming on your campus. We imagine the audience to include students interested in esports; graduate students and faculty members in higher education preparation programs; professionals in academic affairs, intercollegiate athletics, and student affairs; officials in various higher education and intercollegiate associations and governance groups; and other stakeholders in what happens with esports in higher education. It is our hope as the authors of this project to meet the expectations of all of these groups of readers. Many gamers start a game with "GLHF", an abbreviation for "Good luck, and have fun." We wish you the same as you go through this book—GLHF!

ACKNOWLEDGMENTS

The authors—George, Ryan, and Charles—thank David Brightman, Dennis Hall, Peter Lake, and James Stascavage, each of whom served as an important catalyst for this project. Peter Lake invited George to present on ethical and legal issues related to esports in higher education at Stetson University's National Conference on Law and Higher Education (a terrific annual program) and, in doing so, introduced George to Ryan. James Stascavage, in his role shepherding programs for senior student affairs officers (SSAOs) at the NASPA national conference, was kind enough to invite George to take part in the round table discussion for SSAOs on esports in higher education, and it is there that he met Dennis and Charles. Dennis Hall was an early advocate for writing a book on esports, and he graciously and generously shared his experiences, ideas, and insights on the topic during the early stages of the development of the book. David Brightman is exactly the kind of person one wants to have as an editor-partner. He is excited about ideas, practical about book prospects, and thoughtful and honest in his feedback. He is also funny, genuine, and supportive (even when sharing things you may not want to hear). When we broached the idea of this book with David, he immediately saw the need and possibilities for the project, even though, while a growing phenomenon, esports in higher education is still not widely written about. David and Stylus Publishing, LLC, gave us the chance to bring this topic more into the forefront of conversation. We are indebted to him and the team at Stylus for their invaluable support throughout the publication process.

George S. McClellan

I am grateful to Ryan and Charles. They brought a rich array of experiences and insights to the development of this writing project and shared their warmth and good humor in equal measure. One is fortunate to have partners such as these two in any endeavor. I am also grateful to Peggy Barr, James Rhatigan, and Art Sandeen for their invaluable guidance, encouragement, and support in pursuing the role of practitioner-scholar. Hopefully the work does their efforts proud.

I greatly appreciate the support of my colleagues in the higher education department at the University of Mississippi, as well as the students there. Together they help create a caring and thoughtful community focused on important issues of equity, access, affordability, and achievement in higher education. Thanks as well to the folks at the B.B. King Museum, Highway 61 Museum, and all the other historic blues sites in Mississippi. You and the musicians, young, old, and in between, are keeping the blues alive! Finally, a shout out from Lord Widget to Cheese, Gaz, Harry, Ice, Lilac, Monica, Vibber, Zags, Zero, and all the Inglorious Basterds of Lords Mobile.

Ryan S. Arnett

Writing a book at such an early time in my life about a subject I'm passionate about has been fun and fulfilling, and it would not have been possible without a lot of help. I am truly thankful for anyone and everyone who offered words of advice, comfort, guidance, and friendship to me throughout my work on this book. We would be here for a very long time if I listed every person I was thankful for during this time. Just know that your help and guidance did not go unnoticed.

A few people deserve special thanks. I would not have had this wonderful opportunity right out of law school to write on something that I truly care about without the help and belief of George and Charles. This book could not have been done without them. I will be forever grateful to Peter Lake for taking me under his wing during law school and accepting esports as a valid topic to study. Without his guidance and support throughout my time at Stetson University, I would surely not be writing this book now.

I would not be where I was in gaming or esports today without my friends Chris ("Taksee") and Brian ("Bhink"). When I was a new PC gamer, these two showed me the ropes and raised me up to heights that I did not think possible. I would have never had the skills to compete without their help.

I am thankful that my parents, Shawn and Frances, allowed me to continue to play video games as a child and explore my passion. Although it was restricted at times, it could have been a lot worse. A huge thank you to my girlfriend, Shayla, and my husky, Ezekiel. They were my support system through the drafting of this book. They were there for me when things were going great and when things were going not so great. I was able to put myself in front of the screen and type away with their help. Hours spent by my side from Zeke and home-cooked meals from Shayla were just the fuel I needed to keep going.

The biggest thanks of all goes to my grandpa Dennis. Without him, I may have never really discovered my passion for gaming and grown into the man I am today. This book, my passion, and my love for esports and gaming would be nonexistent without him.

Charles M. Hueber

Allow me to first thank my coauthors, George and Ryan, for the many calls and their patience as we sorted through this experience. Having a faculty member, former student, and student affairs professional collaborate on such a project has been a joy. I would also like to give a great deal of credit to my staff at Schreiner University, especially David Gehrels, Matt Goodwyn, and Ryan Lucich. I would have never been able to make any progress without their guidance and help. Thanks also needs to go out to Eric Lambert of Association for the Promotion of Campus Activities, with whom I attended a webinar on esports that inspired a new way of seeing it. Finally, I appreciate my family, who not only gave up their time to allow me to work on this project but also sat through endless dinnertime conversations as I bounced ideas off them.

1

AN OVERVIEW OF ESPORTS IN HIGHER EDUCATION

What Is It, How Big Is It, and How Does It Work?

In *Culture Is Our Business*, Marshal McLuhan (1970) predicted that electronic media would restructure human society into tribes of affiliation. Kozinets (1999), writing nearly 30 years later, pointed to electronic games as offering "an important space from which to examine the intersection of recreational and relational online modes in the creation and collective consumptions of fantasy experience" (p. 262). Now, 50 years after McLuhan's observations and 20 years after those of Kozinets, electronic sports, or *esports* as it is commonly called, offers ample evidence of the prescience of those two scholars. Esports is at the center of a global gaming and business phenomenon (Seo, 2013) that includes wide-scale interest and participation by a diverse array of people.

Among those esports players are college students who, as part of noninstitutional teams as well as teams affiliated with their colleges and universities, spend a great deal of effort and time perfecting their skills and sharing their experiences with virtual networks of other players. A growing number of institutions see esports as presenting opportunities such as increasing enrollment, student learning and development, and institutional prestige. How many students are involved in esports? In what games? What are their experiences in esports? How many institutions are offering esports opportunities? In what forms? How is that working out for them? How are esports organized as a field? Who, if anyone, is governing intercollegiate esports? We will attempt to answer these and other questions about esports and higher education throughout the course of this book.

We begin in this chapter by offering an overview of esports. What exactly is it, and who is competing in it? Who is attending esport events? How are people learning about esports? Who is watching esports and through what means? Is it really a sport? Next, we discuss esports as a business and entertainment enterprise before moving into specifically exploring the big-picture questions about the connection between esports and higher education.

What Is Esports?

It might be helpful at this point to define *esports*. As Funk et al. (2018) wryly observed, "While all eSports are video games, not all video games should be classified as sports" (p. 9). A simple definition is that *esports* are multiplayer video games that are played competitively, often for spectators, either over local area networks (LANs) or online. However, the relatively recent emergence of esports as an international phenomenon, the rapidly changing nature of the underlying technology, the variety of types of games generally included within the field, and the diversity of disciplinary perspectives of those seeking to author a definition all make developing a singular and commonly accepted definition somewhat of a challenge.

Defining Sports

Those seeking to define *esports* commonly begin their effort by offering a definition of sport itself. A number draw on the work of Tiedemann (2004), who defined *sport* as

> a cultural field of activity in which human beings voluntarily go into a real or only imagined relation to other people with the conscious intention to develop their abilities and accomplishments particularly in the area of skilled motion and to compare themselves with these other people according to rules put self [*sic*] or adopted without intending to damage them or themselves deliberately. (p. 3)

Wagner (n.d.) refined Tiedemann's definition of *sport* by highlighting cultural relevance. He offered the following:

> Sport is a cultural field of activity in which people voluntarily engage with other people with the conscious intention to develop and train abilities of cultural importance and to compare themselves with these other people in these abilities according to generally accepted rules and without deliberately harming anybody. (p. 2)

Defining Esports

Working from this definition and noting that in contemporary society technological skills are culturally important, Wagner (n.d.) went on to define *esports* as "an area of sport activities in which people develop and train mental or physical abilities in the use of information and communication technologies" (p. 3).

Hamari and Sjöblom (2017), in somewhat of a departure from Wagner, put the emphasis on "what constitutes the 'e' in esport" (p. 213). For them,

> the crucial question is then what portions or aspects of the sport have to be electronic and/or computer mediated for a sporting activity to be counted as an eSport. We argue that the main difference between a sport and an eSport comes down to where the player or team activities that determine the outcomes of the sport/play are manifested. In traditional sports, all outcome-defining activities can be seen to happen in the "real world," even though the sport's practitioners may employ electronic and computerized systems to aid the sporting activities. However, we observe and argue that in eSports, the outcome-defining activities happen in a "virtual world"; however, it is not the physical and practical circumstances that the player inhabits that ultimately defines the outcome of play, but rather the system states that exist within the confines of the electronic system (which is controlled by the player and governed by the rules of the eSport's software and technology). (p. 213)

Seo (2013) differentiated esports from other electronic gaming practices in that esports "is primarily played to improve consumer abilities in the use of digital technologies and playing computer games as a form of competition" (p. 1544). Seo also noted that

> a computer game played for eSports must feature some objective measures of comparison that can be used to judge players' performances within the game. These measures may and often do vary from one computer platform to another. For instance, in one computer game, players may be required to defeat their opponents, whereas in another game, their performance may be judged according to their gaming score. Furthermore, the rules and formats of competition are often governed by the external governing bodies and communities of eSports players, which now perform an institutionalizing role in ensuring the consistency of conduct among various competitive computer-gaming practices. (p. 1544)

Types of Esports Games

So what games make up esports, and what are those games like? This section offers a typology of the most common forms of electronic games played competitively as esports and offers examples of some of the most popular game titles within each of those forms of games (Gambling Sites, n.d.).

Multiplayer Online Battle Arena Games

Multiplayer online battle arena (MOBA) games are typically contests with two opposing teams made up of individual players. Team sizes vary, but five members is common. The team's objective is to destroy the other team's base, but other goals are sometimes identified (e.g., eliminating all the members of the opposing team).

Individual team members have control of a character in the game, and those characters are known as heroes. The strength and skill sets of heroes can be developed through acquiring experience in the game or through obtaining various game items through wager (chapter 5 includes further discussion of gambling in esports) or conquest (either capturing an item or buying it from the game store using game currency earned through various accomplishments in the game). There are various hero types in the games, and a team will typically have a strategy as to the mix of heroes it employs.

MOBA is a very popular form of esports. Among the most popular MOBA games in esports are Dota 2, League of Legends, Smite, and Heroes of the Storm.

First-Person Shooter

First-person shooter (FPS) games are one of the earliest forms of esports games. They first appeared in the mid-1970s, and their popularity skyrocketed in the 1990s. FPS games are similar to MOBA games in that the common objectives are to eliminate the other players or to capture the base of the other players. FPS games may be played individually against the computer, individually against other players, or individually in what is called co-op, where players work together as part of a squad. Problem-solving or puzzle-solving and strategy (particularly as it relates to selection of weapons and battle gear) are important elements of many FPSs.

A distinguishing feature of FPS games is that players view the game from the perspective of their character (or *avatar*). There are also third-person shooter (TPS) games. Fortnite, which actually has three versions (cooperative, battle royale, and build-your-own-environment), is one extremely popular example of a TPS game.

FPS avatars may be enhanced (or healed) through the addition of resources, skill sets, or characteristics. These enhancements are acquired through activities in the game, wagers, or purchases with game currency earned in the course of play.

FPS games are more popular in the Western market. Top FPS games in esports include Counter-Strike: Global Offensive, Halo, Battlefield, Overwatch, and Call of Duty.

Fighting Games
Fighting games feature two players doing exaggerated or fantastical combat with one another. More realistic fighting games such as those about boxing or wrestling are commonly classified as sports games, discussed later in this section. Some games allow the option for multiple-player combat. Some, but not all, fighting games allow the players to make use of weapons. Unlike MOBA and FPS, fighting games commonly take place in smaller defined spaces.

Players in fighting games select characters with specified characteristics and abilities, including special fighting moves triggered through combinations of keystrokes or controller moves. Contests commonly take place in the form of timed rounds viewed from the side. Street Fighter and Super Smash Bros. are examples of fighting games that are popular in esports.

Real-Time Strategy
In contrast to turn-based strategy games (TBS), in which players alternate turns throughout the course of the game, real-time strategy (RTS) contests allow players to take simultaneous actions (or no action) as they pursue the goals of developing their various game assets for the purposes of beating their opponents' armies, undermining their resources, or capturing their territories. RTS games offer an objective overhead view of the terrain in the player's particular area of the game, with a smaller full-game map available off to the side.

Moss (2017), who credited Dune II producer Brett Sperry with creating the term *real-time strategy game,* pointed out the important distinction between tactics and strategy. He wrote:

> Strategy refers to high-level plans whereas tactics is focused on the finer points of execution of specific objectives. In more explicit video game terms, strategy is building and managing armies from the buildings you add to your base with the resources you mine/harvest; tactics is just the combat stuff, with in-depth battleground mechanics that focus on unit formations and positioning and exploiting terrain features to your advantage.

Real-time strategy usually includes some tactics, but real-time tactics rarely includes strategy mechanics. (para. 4)

Many RTS games are best suited for single-player gaming, but there are some team games as well. StarCraft II is probably the best known RTS team game. Warcraft III, Age of Empires, and World in Conflict are popular RTS single-player esports games.

Sports and Racing

Sports games are arguably the oldest of the esports game forms. William Higinbotham created Tennis for Two in 1958 as a game to be played on an oscilloscope between two players (Reimer, 2005). Since then the form has obviously grown in numerous ways. Today sports and racing games include titles that mirror real-life sports as well as some that take a more imaginary approach.

Sports and racing games are commonly single-player games and increasingly are associated with major sports associations or franchises. Players may orchestrate the actions of a single character or those of an entire team in the game. Racing games include the subcategories of arcade-style, simulation, and kart games.

Sports and racing games are not as popular as some of the other types of games identified here, but they do represent a recognizable set of esports games. FIFA Football/Soccer, Madden, and NBA22K are examples of very popular esports realistic sports games. Rocket League is an interesting sports-type game in that it is a fantasy game in which players use rocket-powered craft to move around balls. Although racing games are not as common as sports games in esports, Forza, Gran Turismo, and NASCAR are examples of racing games that are used for esports competitions.

Miscellaneous

Typologies are rarely perfect; distinctions are rarely fully refined within categories, and the process of categorization inevitably fails to be fully inclusive. Our typology of esports games is no exception. There are a few games that do not fit into any of the major types already identified but are very popular all the same. Most notable among these is Hearthstone: Heroes of Warcraft, a card-based game in which players take turns and use acquired skills and game items to compete with one another.

Esports Understood as Part of the Experience Economy

Seo (2013), drawing on the work of Pine and Gilmore (1998), pointed out that esports is more than simply the competitions themselves. Writing in 1998, Pine and Gilmore described an emerging experience economy—one driven by people interested in taking part in and sharing experiences of one sort or another. Their quadrant model describing the kinds of experiences in which consumers may be interested is represented in Figure 1.1.

Seo (2013) described esports in terms of the experience economy

> not merely as a form of playing computer games but as a complex phenomenon characterized by the confluence of multiple interrelated experiential performances. For instance, apart from playing computer games competitively (escape), esports experience can be amplified by attending esports events (esthetic), learning about esports practices (educational), and watching esports media (entertainment). (p. 1543)

We will pick up on Seo's (2013) point about the broader construct of esports by taking some time to discuss who is playing esports (escape), the ways in which people attend esports events (esthetic), the ways people learn about (train for) esports (educational), and how people watch esports or esports-related media (entertainment).

Figure 1.1. Pine and Gilmore's model of consumer experiences.

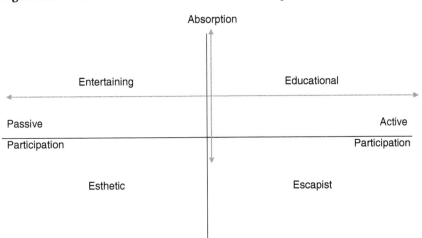

Note. Adapted from Pine & Gilmore (1998).

Who Is Competing in Esports?

Having broadly defined and described esports, we now turn our attention to how many people are competing in esports and who they are. Atari hosted a national Space Invaders competition in 1980 that drew 10,000 participants (Egency, 2018). We have come a long way from that event. It is difficult to find data on the number of people competing in esports worldwide, but data are available for the number of people playing various esports game titles. Table 1.1 presents select data for August 2017.

Although we cannot discern discrete users from the global data, it is reasonable to assert that at least 1 billion people are playing games associated with esports on an annual basis somewhere around the world. Goldman Sachs has estimated the number of monthly esports gamers (those taking part in esports as athletes, attendees at events, or viewers online) to be about 167 million people monthly (Rapoza, 2019), and it seems reasonable to believe that a significant portion of that number are actually participating as athletes in esports. One poll found that 58% of Americans aged 14 to 21 years old reported having played video games competitively (Ingraham, 2018). Other available data from Electronic Entertainment Design and Research (EEDAR) on esports players indicate that 64% of esports players are male and that the average age (which interestingly varies from game title to game title) ranges from 24 to 27 years old (EEDAR, 2015).

TABLE 1.1
Number of Players Worldwide for Selected Esports Games

Game	Players (Millions)
StarCraft II	2.4
PlayerUnknown's Battlegrounds	6.8
Counter-Strike: Global Offensive	11.9
FIFA 17	12.3
World of Tanks	12.3
Dota 2	12.6
Hearthstone	23.9
Call of Duty	28.1
League of Legends	100.0

Note. Adapted from Gough (2017).

There are player data available specific to the United States. About 211 million people in the United States play video games (EEDAR, 2015). A little over one third of those video gamers are aware of esports, and 11% (23 million people) participate in some way. The 23 million individual esports participants include those who compete, attend esports events, or watch esports.

How Many Are Attending Esports Events?

All right. We have some sense of what esports is and of how many people are competing in it. Our next question is how many people attend esports events? Here again, it can be difficult to get precise global data in regard to attendance. That difficulty stems both from the methodological challenges of global data gathering and from concerns regarding data supplied by organizers and promoters of esports events. Nonetheless, we will present what data are available with a caveat to our readers to be mindful of these difficulties.

About 40% of those who play esports indicate that they are likely to attend an esports event (EEDAR, 2015). Of course, not everyone who attends an esports event also plays esports. Family and friends of players, sponsors and their guests, members of the media, curious folks, and others may also attend.

There are a substantial number of esports events taking place every month around the world. These events vary in size from smaller local and regional tournaments to larger national and international events. The top nine esports events in terms of live attendance are shared in Table 1.2.

The demand is such that at least one city in the United States is planning for the construction of an esports arena. The Fusion Arena, a 65,000-square-foot facility, will be home to the Philadelphia Fusion, the city's team in the professional Overwatch League (Tran, 2019). In addition to hosting the team's home events, the arena will also serve as the center for the team's recruitment, training, and regular competitions.

Learning About Esports

We have described esports, the people who compete, and the people who attend events. Continuing with Seo's (2013) framework for understanding esports, how is it that people learn about esports? Who is learning? What about training as a form of learning? We will share information in this section to round out this answer, but a truly exhaustive discussion would take more space than we have here.

TABLE 1.2
Most Attended Esports Events

Event	Location (Year)	Reported Attendance
ESL One/Intel Extreme Masters	Katowice, Poland (2019)	174,000
League of Legends World Final	Beijing, People's Republic of China (2017)	80,000
ESL Dota	Frankfurt, Germany (2015)	52,000
League of Legends World Final	Seoul, South Korea (2014)	45,000
Overwatch League Grand Finals	New York, USA (2018)	20,000
League of Legends World Final	Los Angeles, USA (2013)	12,000
ESL Intel	San Jose, USA (2014)	12,500
League of Legends North American Championship	St. Louis, USA (2019)	10,200
The International	Seattle, USA (2015)	10,000

Note. Information from Bet O'Clock (n.d.); ESL (2019); Murray (2018); Pei (2019).

Online Learning

How are people learning about esports? The quick answer is in lots of ways. A longer answer is through competing and practicing (more on training later in this section). Another answer is through watching esports. Let's talk about how people watch esports and who the people watching are. Here we will note that more than 60% of those people who watch esports online indicate that one of the reasons they do so is to improve their own play. A cursory search on YouTube turns up myriad videos available for those who want to learn more about competing in esports, being a competitor, being an entrepreneur, or the athletes and media celebrities associated with esports. There are also a plethora of websites across the internet offering similar information and a variety of social media feeds to which one can subscribe. Learning about esports, however, is not limited to new media. A quick search of Amazon returns a variety of books ranging from learning how to play to learning how to be an esports entrepreneur.

K–16 Learning

Learning about esports is also not limited to online experiences. There are numerous esports summer camps for children across age ranges.

Esports are now a part of the middle school experience of some students. Knollwood Middle School in Fair Haven, New Jersey, lays claim to the first esports team at a middle school (Bustamante, 2019). The first-ever middle school esports league launched in New York (Kids in the Game, 2019; Newcomb, 2019). Middle school teams and leagues might be new, but esports in middle school is not. We found a 2017 posting by a teacher from James Monroe Middle School in Albuquerque, New Mexico, soliciting donations to support participation in esports by the students at his school (Harvey, 2017). What do educators see as the purpose of making esports opportunities available in middle school? Hennick (2019) described the officials at two schools as wanting "to give their student gamers a chance not only to hone their craft but also to learn how to be team players" (para. 2) and quoted one senior school district official as saying, "What we really want is for the students to come out of the sport knowing how to collaborate, how to communicate, how to value and respect their team members" (para. 2).

Learning about esports also takes place in high schools across the United States. The High School Esports League is one example of a group that promotes the inclusion of esports as part of the curricular and cocurricular offerings of secondary schools (High School Esports League, 2019). It also partners with the National Association of Collegiate Esports in helping move students from competing in esports at the high school level to competing as part of a college or university team. The North American Scholastic Esports Federation (NASEF) is another organization similar to the High School Esports League in its mission and scope (NASEF, 2019). On a much grander scale, the National Federation of State High School Associations (NFHS) partners with online gaming company PlayVS to expand esports opportunities at high schools across the country (NFHS, 2019). The partnership began in 2018. Participating schools field teams that compete in two seasons in a year, playing games approved by the relevant state association. The high schools are required to have faculty advisers and access to the internet. Students taking part in the program pay $16 per month to participate.

We will discuss the intersection of esports and higher education later in this chapter. For now we simply note that esports is a part of the curriculum and cocurriculum at an increasing number of higher education institutions.

Lifelong Learning

Esports is not limited to the span of the K–16 education system. When it comes to esports, learning is very much a lifelong phenomenon. Shacknews, a gaming media company, has recently begun to host the Shack Champions League for players who are more than 30 years old (Brightman, 2018). There is even an interest in esports among chronologically blessed persons. The Silver Snipers from Stockholm, Sweden, sponsored by Lenovo, boast that they are the oldest esports team in the world, with every member being at least 60 years of age (Breshnan, 2019). Athletes competing in these age ranges are no doubt learning and training just as do their junior colleagues.

Training

Training for athletes can be considered a form of learning. The training available to esports athletes is increasing in sophistication as it is informed by the growing body of knowledge available about what it takes to become successful in the sport and to sustain a high level of competitiveness over a period of time. Being an esports athlete can take a significant toll. The hours can be long, stress can be high, and the lifestyle can be isolating, not to mention the demands from coaches, fans, sponsors, and others can draining (Lajka, 2018). As with athletes competing in all sports, training for esports athletes incorporates physical, mental, and nutritional elements (Durrani, 2017; Jacobs, 2015).

The training facility opened in 2018 for Team Liquid, a professional esports team, reflects the advances being made in training for esports athletes (Smith, 2018). The 8,000-square-foot facility in Santa Monica, California, offers players healthy food prepared by a chef on staff, access to coaches, space for game review, and practice facilities (actually, distinct spaces for each of the different teams that Team Liquid fields for various games). The team members have access to a nutritionist and sports psychologist and gym memberships. There is also an on-site video production area to support development of outreach and marketing videos by the athletes. Perhaps most significantly, there are no living quarters, as the older model of a team house has proven to be isolating for esports athletes and to exacerbate stress.

Training opportunities in esports are not limited to the most elite athletes. Higher Level Gaming, an enterprise of the poker media company Card Player, is a company that provides esports training material to a broader audience (Card Player staff, 2019). Their audience comprises athletes new to esports and those with less advanced skills. Gamer Sensei (2019), in contrast, is an example of a company offering online access to skilled esports professionals.GamerSensei's target audience is athletes of average ability who aspire to enhance their skills.

Watching Esports

We now turn our attention to the entertainment aspect of esports (Seo, 2013). That is to say, we consider the experience of people watching esports. Some of our readers may well be wondering whether people really watch this stuff and, if so, how many, and how, and why. This section will address each of those questions.

Number of Viewers

The numbers of people competing in esports and attending esports events are substantial, but they are dwarfed by the numbers of people who watch esports. Literally millions of people watch esports on a regular basis, with the Asian market being the largest (Goldman Sachs, 2019). Nearly 60% of Americans between the ages of 14 and 21 report watching esports either live or via recording (Ingraham, 2018), and one study reports 21% of males 16 to 24 years of age watched an esports tournament in the past month (Buckle & Mander, 2018). Nearly 80% of esports viewers are under 35 years of age (Goldman Sachs, 2019). Over 600,000 watched the North American League of Legends Championship Series Spring Split Finals (Pei, 2019). Table 1.3 presents additional data on viewership for esports tournaments.

Esports viewers, it should be noted, watch more than tournaments. They also watch streamed broadcasts hosted by esports celebrities, well-known esports athletes or popular esports media figures. These streams cover the gamut of esports topics, including what games are hot, tips for better play, news about tournaments, information about athletes, and more (Gallucio, 2019).

Viewing Venues

Although viewers may only occasionally see esports content on cable television (Chapman, 2018; Lingler, 2016) most are watching streamed broadcasts on the internet. Top platforms in the United States for esports streaming are Twitch and YouTube (Buckle & Mander, 2018). How much are people watching on these platforms? The hours of viewership on Twitch in June 2019 for the top esports games are shown in Table 1.4, and the hours of viewership on YouTube in June 2019 for the top esports games are shown in Table 1.5.

TABLE 1.3
Number of Viewers for Select Esports Tournaments

Event	Year	Viewership (Millions)
Mid-Season Invitational	2018	60
Intel Extreme Masters	2017	46
League of Legends World Championship	2016	43
League of Legends World Final	2002	27
Crossfire Stars World Championship	2017	37
League of Legends World Final	2013	32
League of Legends World Championship	2015	36
League of Legends World Final	2002	27

Note. Adapted from Bet O'Clock (n.d.); Gough (2019).

Why Do People Watch?

Why do people watch? According to EEDAR (2015), 70% of those who watch say it is to watch the game being played at a high level, 60% want to improve their own play, and 55% watch when they cannot play. Interestingly, around one third of those who watch say they do so to support a particular team or a particular player (a fact that ought to be of interest to higher education institutions considering streaming their esports teams).

But Is It a Sport?

Readers should have a clear understanding by now of esports and of how significant it is as a social phenomenon. However, there may be some (perhaps more than a few) who are asking themselves whether esports can truly be considered a sport.

In the Affirmative

Addressing esports's status as a sport requires that one begin by defining *sport*. Recall that earlier in this chapter we shared Tiedemann's (2004) definition and Wagner's (n.d.) extension of that definition to incorporate cultural considerations. We have already presented the work of several scholars (Hamari & Sjöblom, 2017; Seo, 2013; Wagner, n.d.) who, using

TABLE 1.4
Hours Viewed by Game on Twitch

Game	Twitch Total Hours (Millions)	Twitch Esports Hours (Millions)
League of Legends	81.4	23.2
Dota 2	41.4	21.5
Overwatch	27.1	16.9
Counter-Strike: Global Offensive	27.3	13.7
Hearthstone	19.3	6.1
Rocket League	4.8	2.7
StarCraft II	4.6	2.2
Call of Duty: Black Ops 4	6.3	2.0
Fortnite	77.5	1.9
Magic: The Gathering Arena	5.9	1.9

Note. Total hours includes all esports content. Esports hours are only those where content was generated by professionally organized esports competitions. Adapted from Newzoo (2019).

the definitions provided by Tiedemann (2004) and Wagner (n.d.), have concluded that esports is a form of sport.

In the Negative

Other scholars, however, have reached a different conclusion. Hallmann and Giel (2018) are representative of those who argue that esports is not a form of sport. They used Rodgers's (1977) four criteria for sports (two required and two ideal) in making their case:

1. It must involve physical activity.
2. It must be practiced for recreational purposes.
3. It should ideally involve an element of competition.
4. It should ideally have a framework of institutional organization.

Hallmann and Giel (2018) specifically cited Hamari and Sjöblom (2017) and argued that their description of esports lacks any reference to physical activity. Although Hallmann and Giel accepted that esports meets the recreational purpose criterion for sports articulated by Rodgers (1977), they contended that the physical activity associated with esports is not of a sufficient level to warrant meeting the first of Rodgers's two required criteria. They did accept that esports involves competition, and they acknowledged some limited organizational structures associated with esports, though they found these to be somewhat lacking in regard to supporting a claim of sports status. Despite their skepticism that esports currently constitutes a form of sport, Hallman and Giel (2018) conceded that "one can argue that eSports is close to but not yet equivalent to sports. However, . . . eSports will likely be officially accepted as a sport" (p. 17).

It has been the experience of the authors that coaches and other professional staff in intercollegiate athletics can be among those at colleges and universities most resistant to accepting esports as a form of sport. Their objections commonly reflect either the arguments made by Hallmann and Giel (2018) or the resistance of the National Collegiate Athletics Association to embrace esports.

TABLE 1.5
Hours Viewed by Game on YouTube

Game	YouTube Total Hours (Millions)	YouTube Esports Hours (Millions)
League of Legends	18.3	8.1
Arena of Valor	4.9	3.1
PlayerUnknown's Battlegrounds	11.9	1.2
Clash Royale	2.6	1.0
Counter-Strike: Global Offensive	6.3	0.7
Tom Clancy's Rainbow Six: Siege	1.5	0.7
Dota 2	4.0	0.6
Fortnite	26.2	0.5
Warface	1.0	0.3
Street Fighter V	0.4	0.3

[a]*Note.* Total hours includes all esports content. Esports hours are only those for which content was generated by professionally organized esports competitions. Adapted from Newzoo (2019).

Our Thoughts

We understand that the question of what constitutes a sport is worth considering as a matter of legal concern. There are ramifications related to licensing, taxation, employment law, and other areas of business operations. The issue of amateurism also arises as a consequence of designating a particular activity as a sport (more on that as it relates to esports and higher education in chapter 6).

We note, too, that there is one significant difference between esports and all the other activities commonly considered to be sports—the issue of ownership. No one owns soccer, football, baseball, track, or water polo. The rules of competition for those activities are decided by their relevant organizing and governing bodies. Esports is different. The games undergirding esports are the intellectual property of the corporate entities holding the rights to those properties. Each entity determines what is offered in the game and what the rules are for play.

That being said, we find ourselves wondering about the extent to which the objection to esports being considered as a sport reflects elitist and ableist notions. Hallmann and Giel (2018) seemed to be asserting that one has to be able to move in certain ways and at certain rates in order for the competitive enterprise in which they are involved to be deemed worthy of designation as a sport.

In the end, we find ourselves in agreement with Funk et al. (2018) on whether esports can rightly be classified as sport. They stated:

> It may take more than consistency with formal definitions to convince sceptics that eSport truly deserves to take a place alongside football, baseball, cricket, and tennis. . . . Lagaert and Rose (2016) contend that an essentialist definition of sport is not possible in any case, as any such definition is necessarily simultaneously both too broad and too narrow, excluding activities that are widely-accepted as sport, while including activities that are not. In their view, a one-size-fits-all definition cannot be developed, in particular because sport itself is a fluid concept and individuals within the sport field compete to assert their preferred interpretations. Ultimately, it may not matter whether eSport is sport. (p. 9)

We are mindful that a similar debate took place in the late 1990s regarding whether or not student affairs had a sufficient philosophical core to allow for it to be counted as a profession (see Bloland et al., 1994). There were thoughtful arguments on both sides of that conversation, but, in the end, what really mattered is that those involved in the field conducted themselves professionally. Over time, the force of their collective effort carried

TABLE 1.6
Revenue Sources by Share of Esports Revenue

Source	2017 (%)	2022 (%)
Sponsorship	38	35
Advertising	22	14
Other	17	7
Media rights	14	40
Tickets/local	9	4

Note. Adapted from Goldman Sachs (2019).

the discussion to a de facto decision. We believe such will be the case with the question of whether or not esports is a form of sport. Whether one accepts esports as sport or not, the obligation of all of us fortunate enough to work with students is to support them in their learning and development regardless of the label we assign to their activity.

Esports as Business

Whatever else one believes about esports, one must accept that it is really big business. Do you recall the typology of forms of esports games shared earlier in this chapter? In terms of sales, the top-grossing game franchises (all versions of a particular game title) as of 2018 for each of the forms are Call of Duty (FPS), $17 billion; Street Fighter (fighting), $11.2 billion; Warcraft (other), $10.6 billion; FIFA (sports and racing), $10.1 billion; League of Legends (MOBA), $8.4 billion; and StarCraft (RTS), $1 billion ("List of highest grossing video game franchises," 2019).

Game sales, however, do not make up the largest share of esports revenue. Table 1.6 shows a breakdown of revenue sources for 2017 and those predicted for 2022.

The financial future of esports, according to Goldman Sachs (2019), will be in media fees and sponsorships. In other words, other big businesses will want to be associated with esports because esports attracts the kinds of customers those businesses seek to cultivate.

Exactly how much money are we talking about? Total esports revenues globally in 2018 were around $1 billion (Rapoza, 2019). The United States and Canada accounted for $409 million of that total and China for another $210 million.

Media

YouTube and Twitch are currently the major platforms for esports media. Of the two, Twitch is a far larger presence. It signed a 2-year deal for streaming rights with the Overwatch League in 2018 reportedly worth $90 million (Fischer, 2018).

Other media companies are looking to make inroads into the marketplace. We have already noted that broadcast television and cable television have not proven to be particularly viable forums for esports. However, a number of the media companies operating broadcast and cable networks have internet-based communications. That is where they see themselves making connections with esports.

Sponsors

As mentioned, sponsorships are a big part of esports business. Sponsors support events, teams, individual players, and broadcasts. The corporations acting as sponsors in esports include some of the largest and most successful companies across a host of business sectors and include both endemic (those who produce goods or services used in esports) and nonendemic brands. Examples of endemic sponsors include Comcast Xfinity, Intel, and Twitch (Egency, 2018; Hayward, 2019; Meola, 2018). Some of the nonendemic sponsoring brands for esports are AT&T, Adidas, Airbus, Audi, BMW, Betaway (gambling platform), Coca-Cola, Domino's, Geico, Honda, KFC, Kia, Kraft Group, Mercedes-Benz, Mobil 1, Monster Energy, Mountain Dew, Puma, New Era, Nike, Nissan, Red Bull, Snickers, State Farm, Tinder, and T-Mobile (Egency, 2018; Hayward, 2019; Meola, 2018).

Professional Sports

One interesting development is the growing number of relationships among various traditional professional sports groups and esports. Although revenue in North America from esports falls well short of that from other major professional sports (the national football and baseball leagues each took in more than $10 billion in 2017, according to Ingraham, 2018), these other sports are paying close attention to the esports world. The National Basketball Association (NBA) was one of the first to see the value of developing esports partnerships. Initial involvement began with investments by NBA owners in various esports enterprises and grew from there to the current partnerships between the NBA itself and the NBA game franchise (Holmes, 2019; Wolf, 2017). Mark Cuban, an owner in the NBA, invested in 2015 in a legal esports betting company, and Stephen Kaplan, co-owner of an NBA team, bought into an esports team in that same year. Not long after, a number of NBA athletes began to invest in esports teams as well. Eventually, the Miami Heat took an ownership position in the Misfits, which competes across a number of esports games. Then, in 2017, the NBA announced it would organize an NBA 2K league. The league has 21 teams, and players are paid a minimum salary of $33,000 for a 6-month contract. That base can be augmented with endorsement deals and prize purses from competitions. There is even a draft for the NBA 2K league much like the draft for the NBA itself.

There is also an eNASCAR Heat Pro League comprising 16 teams, some sponsored by NASCAR racing teams like Richard Childress Racing and Joe Gibbs Racing, and also using a draft (Swerdlow, 2019). The National Football League (NFL) is working with the Madden game franchise on the Madden NFL Championship Series. Major League Soccer (MLS) has eMLS, which is associated with the FIFA eWorld Cup. The National Hockey League (NHL) has the NHL Gaming World Cup Championship. Finally, Commissioner Rob Manfred of Major League Baseball, the only other major professional sports association in the United States not previously mentioned, announced in 2019 that it plans to move forward with building out its esports presence (Strickland, 2019).

Connection Between Esports and Higher Education

Let us review. Esports is a form of sports in which a lot of people from around the world are taking part, including a substantial number of people in North America. The ways in which people are taking part in esports include competing, attending events, learning, and watching programming. Finally, esports is big business—really big.

So what is the connection between esports and higher education? Interestingly, the connection is almost as old as esports itself. One of the first competitions, named the Intergalactic Spacewar Olympics, was held in 1972 on the campus of Stanford University with the grand prize being a year's subscription to *Rolling Stone* magazine (Baugh, 2019). A fair number of college students are participating in esports. Thanks to the interest of those students and of potential students, higher education is discovering esports, and the interest appears to be reciprocal. Esports companies began offering college scholarships as early as 2016 (Weller, 2016). Chris Hopper, who heads League of Legends publisher Riot Games, said,

> We're thinking through ways to build out our competitive pipeline beyond just the [League Championship Series]. . . . As a kid growing up, I had countless

leagues and clubs to play soccer or basketball or baseball, and we think that our work in building out the collegiate competitions and scholarship offers, as well as our partnership with PlayVS to make League of Legends an official high school varsity sport, will pay great dividends in the future. (quoted in Pei, 2019, para. 13)

How Many Institutions Are Involved in Esports?

It can be difficult to say precisely how many colleges and universities offer esports programs at any given moment, for two reasons. First, the numbers are changing rapidly. Second, there is no single repository for the information or authoritative research on which to rely. We estimate that in early 2019 approximately 500 higher education institutions offered esports programs in the form of club teams or varsity intercollegiate athletics (McClellan & Arnett, 2019; Next College Student Athlete [NCSA], 2019). No information is currently available on how many more institutions may offer esports in the form of recognized student organizations (RSOs). These institutions span the North American continent and include 2-year and 4-year institutions; religiously affiliated, technical, and liberal arts; metropolitan and rural; in athletic associations and not in associations; and public and private institutions. A good number of the institutions offering esports programs are small to medium-sized institutions with modest selectivity profiles, but larger institutions are also involved. Some see esports as a vehicle that allows smaller institutions and less well-known institutions to compete with larger and more widely recognized ones (Keeler, 2018).

Why Are Institutions Involved in Esports?

Although there is no published research yet on what motivates colleges and universities to develop esports programming, we believe the following to be among the most common purposes (with enrollment being the strongest of the motivations and the rest listed in no particular order):

- Strengthening enrollment (recruiting and retention, particularly of males)
- Creating revenue streams (cultivating new sponsors, donors, and partners)
- Fostering student development and learning (both curricular and cocurricular)

- Expanding student career opportunities (e.g., introducing, encouraging, and supporting students in game design or esports management)
- Increasing institutional recognition/prestige (through team competitiveness; association with current technological, commercial, and entertainment developments; or connection to nationally and internationally recognized brands)
- Enhancing institutional image (esports programming as symbolic of being innovative, modern, and inclusive)
- Shifting campus culture (emphasizing that athletic and intellectual pursuits are both valued and that all sorts of students can represent the university)
- Adding intercollegiate athletic and club team opportunities available for all genders

There are other ways to pursue these same outcomes. So why are colleges and universities looking to esports? The answer may be, at least in no small part, money. There are dollars available from donors, partners, and sponsors to help support program development in this area. In addition to the perception that there is money out there, esports are also seen as comparatively inexpensive when compared to other initiatives that might be undertaken for the same purposes (Hennen, 2019).

Esports Programming at Colleges and Universities

Higher education is expanding its approach to esports "beyond the screen and into academic opportunities" according to Zimmerman (2018, para. 4). Esports programming in higher education can be described as taking place as part of either the curriculum or cocurriculum.

> Student experiences, including learning and development, are shaped by both what goes on inside their college or university and outside of it. The internal activities, meaning those which are formally and legally functions of the college or university, may be understood as either curricular or cocurricular in nature. (Sun & McClellan, 2019, p. 55)

Of course, in a robust learning environment, these two areas of activity are purposefully and thoughtfully interconnected.

Curriculum
The curriculum includes those activities "directly associated with the specified academic functions of the institution—specific courses and classes;

majors and minors leading to degrees; grading and advancement policies; and required internships or practicum are all examples of elements of the curriculum" (Sun & McClellan, 2019, p. 55).

MIT's inclusion of an esports panel for several years at their Sloan Sports Analytics Conference is an example of an academic presentation outside the structure of a course or credential program. So too is the summer Esports 101 course offered by the University of Oregon's Warsaw School of Sports Marketing in partnership with Turner Sports. Syracuse University also worked with an industry partner, Twitch, in developing its esports curriculum (Reames, 2018). Miami University, University of Nevada, Las Vegas, and University of South Carolina are just a few of the colleges and universities with courses addressing esports (Funk et al., 2018). Becker College offered the first bachelor's degree in esports management. Emerson College, University of California at Irvine, and Shenandoah University are examples of higher education institutions offering undergraduate courses in this area (Zimmerman, 2018).

Ohio State University is planning an interdisciplinary esports program that will span its engineering, education and human ecology, arts and sciences, business, and medicine colleges. It will include design and production content and offer undergraduate and graduate degrees as well as certificates. The program will be housed in a 4,000-square-foot facility that will include an 80-seat esports arena. The facility will also be home to the institution's varsity esports team (Busta, 2018; Zimmerman, 2018).

Cocurriculum
The cocurriculum includes

> those programs, practices, and services made available through the college or university to its students for the purpose of enhancing student learning and development and which are intended to augment and supplement the institution's curricular offerings. Student organizations, campus housing, intercollegiate athletics, and campus conduct codes and processes are all examples of co-curricular student life. (Sun & McClellan, 2019, p. 56).

Cocurricular esports offerings at colleges and universities commonly take one of three forms: RSOs, club teams, or intercollegiate varsity athletics. Each of the three will be addressed in this section.

RSOs present the simplest and quickest way for esports to be added to the cocurriculum. Driven by student interest and organized by students, the recognition process for student organizations on most campuses often takes a few weeks to a month or so. Most institutions require that an RSO has a staff or faculty adviser and that the officers of the RSO agree to be responsible for ensuring that the student group adheres to the required policies and practices of the host institution. RSO status typically affords the group access to campus room reservations, campus vehicle reservations, and the opportunity to apply for funding. RSOs are official entities of the host institution and so may make use of the college or university name within institutional guidelines. An esports RSO is an attractive option for students who want to come together with fellow students at their college or university to enjoy competing with one another in esports and learning from one another about esports.

Club teams are a particular form of RSO in that they are created with the express purpose of competing with other clubs, at higher education institutions or elsewhere, in a particular sport. The recognition process is similar to that for RSOs; an adviser is commonly required, and student leaders agree to be responsible for the club team's compliance with institutional rules and guidelines. Institutional support for club team athletes is limited if available at all. Club team student-athletes do not receive athletic scholarships from their college or university.

Varsity intercollegiate athletics are organized and managed by the higher education institution itself, unlike RSOs and club teams that are student-managed programs. Student-athletes competing in varsity intercollegiate athletics may receive athletic scholarships. Colleges and universities in the United States involved in intercollegiate athletics commonly belong to one of three member-driven governance associations: the National Association of Intercollegiate Athletics (NAIA), the National Collegiate Athletic Association (NCAA), or the National Junior College Athletic Association (NJCAA). Both NAIA and NJCAA are partners with the National Association of Collegiate Esports (NACE), a membership organization that promotes intercollegiate esports and helps organize leagues. The NCAA has yet to partner with NACE as the NCAA has concerns regarding the issue of amateurism as it relates to esports (an issue addressed in more detail in chapter 6).

Colleges and universities may also compete in intercollegiate athletics, including esports, as part of a league, or they may stand as independent competitors. Although not sanctioned by the NCAA, 12 of the 14 members of the Big Ten conference have partnered with Riot Games (the publishers of League of Legends) and the Big Ten Network to stream a season of competitions (Rovell, 2017).

Robert Morris University (Moore, 2017) was the first university to offer athletic scholarships to esports players in 2014 when it offered scholarships in two tiers—35% of tuition and 70% of tuition. The University of Pikeville, Maryville University, Southwestern University, and Columbia College are examples of other institutions that also began offering such scholarships around that time. In a first-of-its-kind event, the University of Utah added a varsity esports program in 2017, becoming the first school from one of the Power Five conferences to do so (University of Utah, 2017). Marquette University purports to be the first NCAA Division I institution with an esports program housed within its athletics department (Bauer-Wolf, 2019). Today there are about 200 colleges and universities offering varsity scholarships to esports athletes, with a value of roughly $15 million per year (an amount that more than tripled between 2015–2016 and 2018–2019), with the average scholarship being worth around $5,000 (Heilweil, 2019).

Colleges and universities with varsity esports programs offer training and competition facilities for their athletes, as well as scholarships, coaches, and trainers. Facilities may range from fairly modest converted spaces (a former classroom or computer lab) to specially designed suites of rooms (Liu, 2019). Some institutions with varsity intercollegiate programs have also created spectator venues where fans can cheer their team on during competitions. The University of California at Irvine in 2016 took the step of being the first public research university with an esports arena (University of California, Irvine, 2016).

Organizational Structure

Although recent data are not available, one report has noted that, among NACE members, 47% of esports programs are located within student affairs, 40% within athletics, and 13% within academic affairs (Bauer-Wolf, 2019). Chapter 2 will offer insights and advice about establishing a successful esports program, including how to decide where the program ought to be placed within the institution's organizational structure.

As an important additional note regarding esports programming in higher education, much more takes place on campuses than what is officially recognized and organized through the formal curriculum and cocurriculum. When it comes to esports, there can be established and well-recognized individual athletes and teams of athletes operating on campuses even before (or even while) the institution has made a conscious decision to engage in esports programming.

Who Is Providing Guidance and Governance?

One of the strengths of American higher education is its guidance and governance systems. Standards for programs and services, including ethical principles to guide decision-making, are promulgated by disciplinary, professional, and sports associations as well as accrediting entities. Procedures, including processes for thoughtful review and inclusive discussion, are established and clearly understood.

Tespa and the National Association of Collegiate Esports (NACE) currently serve to provide guidance for colleges and universities interested in or involved in esports. Both are membership-driven organizations.

Tespa, formerly known as the Texas eSports Association, was founded at the University of Texas, Austin, in 2012 as a campus gaming group. Tespa entered into a partnership with Blizzard Entertainment (publisher of several esports game titles) to support expansion of the organization ("Tespa," 2019). Today Tespa has over 270 chapters and more than 100,000 registered players and alumni from across Canada and the United States (Tespa, 2019). Of those, about 28,000 are registered players (Heilweil, 2019). The organization promotes esports in higher education, helps members organize leagues, and offers its own competitions. Tespa leagues and competitions make use of the games published by Blizzard Entertainment. Tespa claims to be the largest operator of collegiate esports leagues, with more than 1,200 colleges and universities having competed in their tournaments, where about $3 million in scholarship prizes have been awarded. It works in partnership with Twitch and ESPN, among others (Tespa, 2019).

Like Tespa, NACE is a membership organization. For purposes of expediency, NACE was originally chartered as a subsidiary of the NAIA, and it is in the process of becoming an independent not-for-profit organization, according to Michael Brooks, NACE executive director (personal communication, 2019). It currently has around 150 colleges and universities as members (National Association of Collegiate Esports, 2019a). Its focus is on colleges and universities interested in or already competing in intercollegiate varsity esports. It offers information on how to set up programs, a job listing portal, and discussion space for higher education professionals (athletic directors, coaches, and others) to talk about esports. NACE claims to have distributed $15 million in scholarship prizes at its tournaments that feature a number of games from different publishers (National Association of Collegiate Esports, 2019a). NACE notes the following as being among the titles used by its members in competition: Apex Legends, Counter Strike, FIFA, Fortnite, Hearthstone, League of Legends, Madden, NBA 2K, Overwatch, Paladins, Rainbow Six, Rocket League, Smite, and Super Smash Bros. (National Association of Collegiate Esports, 2019b). NACE lists a number of partners on its website. Two of particular interest are BeRecruited and Next College Student Athletes, both involved in helping institutions recruit esports student-athletes. As noted previously, both the NAIA and the NJCAA are also NACE partners. The High School Esports League, also mentioned previously in the chapter, is included among NACE's associates.

Neither Tespa nor NACE began as governance organizations. NACE took steps to become a governance organization at its 2019 national conference. Those steps will be described and discussed in greater detail in chapter 5.

Conclusion

Hopefully we have provided readers with information about esports and its connection to higher education that answered questions and raised some as well. Moving ahead, chapters 2 and 3 will address how to establish and maintain successful esports programs across a variety of institutional types and settings. Chapter 4 will discuss esports from the perspective of the student-athlete. Ethical and legal concerns for consideration in collegiate esports programs will be addressed in chapter 5, and chapter 6 will highlight important themes from throughout the book as well as point us toward the future of esports in higher education.

2

CREATING A SUCCESSFUL ESPORTS PROGRAM ON CAMPUS

Higher education is in a liminal period that is being driven in no small part by changing demographics and technology. More and more, colleges and universities are looking for ways to survive, let alone to grow. Jeffery Docking, in *Crisis in Higher Education: A Plan to Save Small Liberal Arts Colleges in America*, outlined an aggressive approach he claimed would not merely provide a bump in enrollment but create a significant sustained gain (Docking & Curton, 2015). His main argument was students are increasingly making choices about which college they should attend based on what extra or cocurricular programs are available to them.

There has been notable growth in the variety of options students have as colleges are scrambling to play catch-up. Institutions are constantly adding more programs to attract new students and provide a compelling reason to keep students from leaving or transferring out. Higher education will need to be creative and flexible as we look to design programs that will meet the needs of our students and achieve the desired outcomes established by our institutions. In this way our challenge is not to think outside of the box but to build a bigger box. Esports, which is situated at the intersection of new demographics and technology, can help us do that.

We have long known that addressing students' social integration through programming can impact both recruitment and retention. Theoretically, such programs should help in part because they foster integration into campus communities and help align personal goals with institutional goals (Astin, 1984). Esports can provide just such an opportunity to intentionally create and strengthen a connection between students and the institution.

The growth of esports in higher education began as a grassroots movement of students across the nation forming ad hoc teams and organizing themselves to meet their needs. More recently, colleges and universities are creating esports programs or planning to start esports programs. Doing so presents a unique opportunity to meet students on their turf and provide structure while strengthening connections between students and the institution.

College presidents are scrambling to launch esports programs and connect them to their universities in meaningful ways as the market demand for these opportunities explodes. Colleges and universities will face a number of challenges in launching a fully supported and managed program. If it is done correctly, however, it will provide a structured way for all students (on campus, off campus, and online) to engage in a program that can provide measurable learning outcomes and has been proven to have a positive impact on retention rates.

This chapter offers general recommendations and outlines a process for colleges and universities considering adding an esports program. The information shared is broad enough that it could be helpful to any institution, but readers are encouraged to tailor and scale what is presented to meet the circumstances and needs of their own campus. The chapter opens with three foundational steps in laying the groundwork for exploring the addition of esports programming. Seven questions that ought to be addressed as part of a feasibility study to inform decision-making are also described in some detail. Discussion then turns to the importance of identifying leadership for a new esports program, followed by advice for building a successful and inclusive esports program. The importance of linking esports programs to the academic mission of the institution and the development and assessment of learning outcomes as an important strategy in the effort are presented next. The chapter then turns to planning for facilities to support cocurricular esports programming before moving on to concluding thoughts.

Three Foundational Steps

The addition of programs like esports comes at a cost, and a college needs to critically examine all options fully before making the leap. Three important steps in helping ensure an exploratory process that serves the interests of students and the institution are: building a table and inviting the right folks to it, planning for the time to do a thorough job, and conducting a feasibility study. Each of these steps is discussed in greater detail in this section.

Building a Table and Inviting the Right Folks to It

An important consideration is identifying or creating a venue through which the institution can explore its interest in esports. Too often colleges and universities rush to create a new structure for their new idea; we strongly advise that the first effort be consideration of any existing and accepted venue that will meet the needs for exploring esports. Doing otherwise runs the risk of alienating folks invested in shared governance and may generate unnecessary resistance for new ideas (McClellan & Hutchens, in press). Create an ad hoc group only if it is determined there is no extant entity that will meet the needs of the task at hand.

What are those needs that should be met by the venue for exploring the possibility of esports programming? They are those that would inform almost any decision-making process intended to be effective and inclusive. Make sure that all those with an interest have a seat at the table or a way to be heard at the table. Bring requisite expertise to the discussion. Be sure that those who can help make things happen are either at the table or have significant seconds at the table. Include those who might be skeptical or have a reason to be concerned or opposed to the idea in question; their voices are important too.

What might all of this look like when it comes to the exploration of esports programming? Most importantly, make sure that students who currently engage in gaming on campus participate in this process—this is critical to its success. Do you have any faculty or staff members who are esports enthusiasts or players? Invite one or more of them if you do. Include representatives from academic affairs, student affairs, and athletics, as these are the organizational units where the various components of an esports program might be housed. Invite faculty members from departments where esports content might be a part of the curriculum or become a part of the curriculum, as well as a representative of the student affairs committee of the faculty governance group on campus and the faculty athletics representative. Someone from financial affairs could offer insight into questions related to budget and the management of resources. It is important to have a member of your information technology (IT) staff on the committee as they will be able to help answer questions you have not considered. If they are involved early on in this process, they will be more likely to be willing to help when you really need them. Although it may not be necessary to have them represented at the table, it is likely the group will want to hear at some point from the institution's development office, any businesses that might have an interest, and other community parties who could provide useful information or support.

Planning for the Time to Do a Thorough Job

It seems to us as authors that there are few things more costly than hurried decisions. That can certainly be the case when it comes to getting esports programming off the ground at a college or university. It may feel to some on your campus that you are coming late to the party and that there is a need for urgency lest your college or university lose out on an opportunity. If, as the authors believe, esports is here to stay in higher education, then there is enough time to get things right. You want to have a solid plan in place and broad buy-in from your community to avoid major setbacks.

Plan to take the time to collect important data to inform any decisions. How much do you know about the level of student activity and interest in esports at your campus? Where and in what ways are esports already being addressed in the curriculum? What will your existing technology infrastructure support, and what will it take to get that infrastructure to where you would like it to be for the esports program you aspire to create? What are other institutions (both secondary and postsecondary) doing in regard to esports that might offer opportunities for creative collaboration, competition structures, or competition in the marketplace for students or potential sponsors? These are just some of the questions your exploratory group may wish to consider for which data may need to be gathered.

Time is required to not only develop a set of recommendations but also guide any proposals through the appropriate processes, including those related to shared governance.

Conducting a Feasibility Study

Knowing why your institution might want to add esports programming allows the school to take the next step in the process—conducting a feasibility study to help decide whether you can achieve those goals. Asking the right questions before investing resources into a program is fundamental to the success of the program. There are many resources out there to help schools start esports programs and complete feasibility studies specific to your campus. The time and money you save by having an expert come in and help you set up a program the right way will pay off.

This section of the chapter focuses on seven questions that ought be addressed in a feasibility study for esports programming on campus.

Why Is Your School Interested in Esports?

In chapter 1 we discussed the motivating factors that a college may have when establishing an esports program. It is important at the front end to clearly articulate the goals being pursued to help ensure programming is designed to support pursuit of those goals. You may have heard this analogy, but it bears repeating. In higher education, we are often guilty of shooting arrows at a blank wall and, after the shots are taken, drawing a target around our arrows and patting ourselves on the back for a job well done. To assess programs correctly, and in our case launch one successfully, we must draw the target first.

A very important point that should be addressed is the possible opportunity to grow enrollment via esports through the recruitment of students who would not have otherwise chosen the college and the increased retention of students who are currently enrolled. As esports further establishes itself as a legitimate collegiate program, more and more students may choose a college based on the opportunity to participate in an esports program, as they do with other sports and activities.

This section of the feasibility study should include information gathered from across campus through interviews or surveys. The goal is both to measure and generate interest. If you have formed a committee for this task, that committee should interview the following people on campus about their desire or interest in esports programming on campus: president, chief academic affairs officer, chief student affairs officer, chief financial officer, chief information officer, and student body president. Each of these individuals will have critical insight as you move forward in this process.

After speaking to senior-level administrators, you might consider conducting a survey to gain a broader perspective from across campus. A survey can help provide valuable data that could enhance the case to establish a program. One college sent a simple survey to all faculty, staff, and students asking them to rank a list of possible new programs and included esports on that list. What they found was overwhelming support for the addition of esports from across campus.

Input may also be gathered from important constituents outside the institution. Are there businesses or other local groups that might have an interest in seeing esports programming come to the college or university? If so, what is it that they are looking for as a result? Skilled employees? Boost to day tourism? Impacting perception of livability in the local community? Marketing connections with their products or services?

What Is the Level of Involvement of Current Students in Esports?

An important part of beginning any formal esports programming on campus is understanding that esports are probably already present on campus. College students have been engaged in competitive esports at varying levels for over a decade. Colleges are just playing catch-up and only recently realizing a benefit to connecting to these students.

The key to this section of your study is identifying the students on your campus who are fans of or participants in esports to gain a better understanding of the esports culture that has organically evolved on your campus and what direction it has taken. You are looking to establish current interest and participation that can guide you as you start to design and build a sustainable program.

Is Esports Right for Your School?
To what degree would esports programming, curricular or cocurricular, align with the mission, vision, and values of your institution? Will esports programs have natural linkages to other institutional efforts, or will they be isolated in some way?

Many of the curricular elements of esports programming are professional in nature. Does your college or university engage in professional education programs, or would this be a first? Simply being the first does not mean that it would not be aligned, but it cannot simply be assumed to be the case without thoughtful deliberation.

A great deal of research on violence, aggression, brain chemistry, and antisocial behavior in the video game industry exists, and this section can provide an opportunity to investigate these and other issues. Is your institution willing to move forward knowing about these challenges? If so, are there responsibilities that you believe you have as a result? Can your institution do something to define its esports programming to avoid being part of any aspects of esports that are not consistent with norms of the institution? Chapter 5 discusses these issues in further detail and highlights the importance of ensuring that a new program aligns with institutional values.

Do You Have What It Takes to Be Successful?
One of the greatest hurdles a college may face in launching esports is its ability to make the resources (space, funding, and human capital) available to be successful. The cost of adding a new program is not to be taken lightly; any request to support esports programming is likely to be competing with ideas for funding other new (and arguably equally worthy) programs. Often the decision to add funding will require pulling funding from or limiting funding to another area or program. This should only emphasize the importance of doing all of your homework when building a budget to ensure you are providing the very best information.

Start-up costs are resources you will need to have in place before you begin esports program operation. Work on a start-up cost estimate that can help guide the decision-making in this process and provide relevant information for your administration. Start-up costs associated with curricular esports programs are not all that unlike similar costs for other new academic programs. You may have expenses for searching for faculty or staff and for relocating them to your campus. There will be expenses associated with preparing their work spaces, and there may be expenses to create appropriate lab or classroom spaces. Start-up costs for cocurricular programming, including the creation of an esports arena, will be covered later in this chapter. A good model to follow for costs associated with a varsity esports program would be the start-up costs of one of your current athletic programs like soccer or basketball. Here again, you should reach out to other colleges that have recently begun a program and ask them to share their experiences with start-up costs.

It is also important to identify the first-year operating costs. The categories of expense associated with cocurricular varsity esports programs are not all that different from those for other sports, but there are some particular aspects of those expenses that merit discussion here, as there may be questions about them.

- *Travel.* Yes, you should travel with a team. We would suggest at least two off-site tournaments a year. An esports program will not need to travel as much as a basketball program, and one of the benefits of esports is that players do not need to travel to play. However, students will see a huge benefit by participating in programs that have a travel component.
- *Equipment.* You will need to include this in operating expenses, as you will have replacement parts that will be needed annually. You should talk to your IT team about how they budget for a replacement cycle for computers on campus, but you should also consider the peripherals. A keyboard, mouse, and gaming headset used several hours each day can wear out fairly quickly.
- *Uniforms.* Esports branded jerseys are one of the perks students are looking for, and they can and should have a wow factor.
- *Membership fees.* Competition, as in NCAA sports, is not free. Organizations like NACE and Tespa offer online competitions, whereas a new group, the Student League for Intercollegiate Esports, offers online, regional, and national competitions. Most of these groups charge membership fees of some sort.
- *Recruiting.* You need a separate line to cover travel for the coach to visit high schools and gaming tournaments to recruit.

- *Salaries.* You will need money to pay a full-time head coach. This program will and can have a huge impact and should be treated like another major program. We are strong advocates for a full-time position here. This person will be asked to manage and juggle many responsibilities. Having this as an added duty to an existing position will divide that person's focus.

Another consideration you will need to address is the source of funding. College budget dollars will need to be invested, but most schools will be hesitant to invest in a new program when nearly all of us are having to make cuts. You should schedule a meeting with your advancement office to gauge the possibility of donors, alumni, and/or friends of the college who could provide start-up costs or support for an esports program. You have the possibility of offering businesses and donors exposure to your events via online streaming, and you might be surprised how many donors have a specific interest in technology initiatives. All efforts should be made to seek outside funding to help support your program. This would include an ongoing plan to have fundraisers to help support the team on an annual basis.

Can You Successfully Recruit Students to Esports Programs?
One of the ways a college can and should justify the addition of esports programming is based on the ability to recruit new students who would not have otherwise chosen to attend. If you can show an improvement in retention as a result of participation in a program, you will strengthen your case, but the real power lies in a program's ability to recruit.

This section of your feasibility study should discuss opportunities on a national, state, and local scale that address the viability of a pipeline that can help the school recruit students to your programming. The number of high school students participating in esports competition is staggering. Some estimates have the number of gamers in the United States under the age of 18 at 42 million (Entertainment Software Association, 2019). Football, which represents the largest high school sport, has just over 1 million (National Federation of State High School Associations, 2019).

A major difference between traditional sports, such as football or basketball, and esports is how they are organized. Esports is still emerging. More high schools are offering esports, but it is still behind the more organized programs like baseball or soccer. This presents a challenge in recruiting when you do not have a clearly identified pool of recruits. This challenge should ease as the National Federation of State High School Associations (NFHS) increases its presence in esports and as state governance groups with authority to sanction high school athletics increasingly recognize esports; both actions will likely lead to more accessible and thorough lists from which to build recruiting efforts for players.

Curricular esports programming can also be a means for recruiting students. Highlighting esports content in fields like marketing, business administration, or computing and game design can attract students with career interests in these areas. Short courses and certificate programs can also attract returning learners seeking additional credentials and skills for career change or career advancement. These markets should be considered as part of this section of a feasibility study.

Can You Create a Reasonable Competition Schedule?
This section of your study should be an examination of the opportunities your club or varsity esports programs will have to compete with other colleges in and beyond your area. You should know how many of the institutions in your peer group have programs and if they exist at the club or varsity level. The landscape for competition is expanding. NACE, Tespa, Collegiate Starleague (CSL), the American Collegiate Esports League (ACEL), and the Student League for Intercollegiate Esports (SLICE) are examples of for-profit and not-for-profit entities supporting the development of various competition structures. There are others popping up every day, and hopefully the competition landscape will continue to become more robust and offer a variety of levels of competition to fit colleges' individual profiles.

What Is the Expected Return on Investment?
As the question of return on investment (ROI) gets at the heart of the financial viability of any proposed new program, it will likely be one of the most scrutinized portions. The calculations themselves seem straightforward, but arriving at the proper numbers with which to complete the calculations can be complex. We recommend that you consult several offices on campus to help achieve the correct figures.

The precise formula used to calculate ROI varies across colleges and universities. A typical model and descriptions of each of the variables in the formula follow:

Expected New Enrollment × (Total Tuition and Fees − Discounts/Scholarships) − (Program Operating Costs + College Operating Costs)= Anticipated ROI

Expected New Enrollment (ENE). This is the total expected new enrollment for both the curricular and cocurricular offerings. These are students that the institution would likely not have otherwise attracted. Typically, sports have a minimum and maximum roster size, and a coach will sit with an athletic director to determine a recruitment goal each year to fill the roster. For esports this is difficult to calculate but should be based on what a college believes its competition schedule will be and what games will be involved. As an example, if you offer League of Legends (5 versus 5), Overwatch (6 versus 6), Smash Bros. (2 versus 2), and Rocket League (3 versus 3), you could have a starting lineup of 16 players; you would need to include space for substitutes and you might even want to field A and B teams. It would not be unusual to have 40 or more students in a varsity esports program.

Total Tuition and Fees (TTF). Colleges will define this very differently, but you should include the total price of attendance with all mandatory fees. This might best be understood as the sticker price as opposed to the net cost as deductions from revenue due to discounts and scholarships are accounted for elsewhere in the calculation.

Discounts/Scholarships (D/S). This includes any anticipated reductions in the stated tuition. Most institutions are aware of their average discount rate, and that rate can be applied to the tuition (and fees if they are also included in calculation of the average discount rate) to reach a reasonable estimate. This figure also includes any scholarships awarded from institutional funds but does not include any scholarships awarded from donated funds.

Program Operating Cost (POC). This is the calculated operating cost for the entire program and should include everything from salaries to travel and fees.

College Operating Cost (COC). This is a calculation of the standard operating costs such as paying faculty/staff, administrative costs, utilities, and other costs associated with running a college and is a per student estimate. This varies from college to college and generally can be calculated between 15% and 20% of the total revenue per student.

Figure 2.1 walks through a fictitious example from a small college where the average discount rate for students is 40% of total tuition and fees, and college operating costs are estimated at 20% of total tuition and fees for new revenue programs.

Figure 2.1. Example of an ROI calculation.

ENE × (TTF − D/S)	=	Anticipated Revenue	−	(POC + COC)	=	Anticipated ROI
20 × ($35,000 − $14,000) =		$420,000	−	($90,000 + $84,000)	=	$246,000

The annual ROI once you have a full roster should be $246,000. It should be noted that the calculation of the ROI in the first year should also deduct the start-up costs. In addition, you may not yet have new students; you might begin the program with students who were coming to the institution otherwise, though you might decide to hold off on actually beginning programming until you are positioned to bring new students into the institution as a result.

Calculating an ROI is not an exact science. You should include your institutional research office, accounting staff, and chief financial officer in this process as you explore these numbers. It might also help to bring in an outside consultant to help with the ROI and/or your feasibility study, so you are confident that you have it correct.

Completing an entire feasibility study may not be necessary, but it can provide you with a framework, so do your homework before you choose to launch a program. What you will find in the course of answering the questions in the study can and will lead you to other questions. Some programs are launched over a summer and others can take a year or more. It is worth repeating that a key to success is being deliberate and involving as many people as possible.

Identifying the Right Students, Staff, and Faculty to Lead Esports Programming

Once you have completed a feasibility study and received the green light to move forward in launching esports programming, you will need to identify the key people needed to get this all started. How you handle this at the beginning can save you a great deal of time and money in the long run.

The Law of the Few

Malcolm Gladwell (2000), in *The Tipping Point: How Little Things Can Make a Big Difference*, posited that "the success of any kind of social epidemic is heavily dependent on the involvement of people with a particular and rare set of social gifts" (p. 33), an idea he calls the law of the few. Colleges and universities wishing to launch successful curricular and cocurricular programming would do well to keep Gladwell's observation in mind as they move forward in identifying students, staff, and faculty to lead their new esports programs.

Let the Students Own It

Esports is and has been inherently social and is driven by an individual's desire to participate. If we can create a connection for individual students to the institution through participation in esports, we will have a positive impact on retention. We have already mentioned the impact on recruiting. You will need to seek the help of select students currently involved on your campus to impact this on any large scale. The difficulty comes in identifying these students and then persuading them to help establish these connections.

The goal will be to identify a group of students who are connectors on campus in terms of esports and who seem to know everyone. These students tend to be the first names that come to mind when you mention esports. In addition to students themselves, colleagues in student activities or campus recreation are the best staff on campus to help identify these connectors. This can be critical early on and will help you as you look to get established.

The most difficult and possibly frustrating task once you identify these connectors will be to allow the students to take ownership. Esports has been a vibrant subculture for years, but now a shift is occurring in which esports is moving to mainstream acceptance. Haenfler (2004) explained that subcultures often arise as a form of resistance to societal norms. The concept of college-sponsored esports is conformist in nature. Therefore, some students in esports may look askance at college or university involvement in their gaming. If staff involved seek or take credit for all these ideas and attempt to push their thoughts on esports, the students who do try to be involved will never truly buy in and take charge of the program. Staff and faculty may not be seen as cool enough to accomplish this task, but with the right direction we can support and guide students as they show us how to build a program.

An initial step is to meet with a small group of the student connectors you have identified and attempt to accomplish two things. First, determine the current status of esports on your campus. Second, start to dream about what an ideal esports program can look like. You should begin to sketch out a rough structure of a program with the students. Later in this chapter we will discuss pulling more students together to help build a truly inclusive model that offers opportunities to a large number of students.

Find the Right Adviser or Coach
The selection of an adviser or coach for an esports RSO, club team, or varsity team is crucial to the group's success. Students involved in RSOs or club teams typically select their own adviser or coach. The college or university can be helpful to students in that process by encouraging them to consider what it is that they are looking for in that role and then helping them reflect on how they might go about identifying someone with the desired attributes to help them with their organization.

Colleges and universities are responsible for selecting coaches to provide leadership in varsity esports programs. We have a tendency to look for an expert in gaming or someone who excels at a particular game. We would warn you against this approach. You want someone who has a passion for esports and has a basic understanding of it; however, primary goals at most higher education institutions relate to student recruitment, retention, and learning. You will be better served hiring a coach who has an understanding of how to connect with students and support their success and who also has an understanding of how colleges work, particularly given that early in the program the coach is likely to have to build a lot of awareness and make connections across campus with partner departments. You will need someone who has enough experience with esports to speak the language, but they will not need to be a professional gamer. Your coach will need to be willing to work late hours to match student schedules, be flexible, and be able to communicate clearly to potential students, staff, and faculty colleagues. Do not forget interactions with the families of potential and current students as part of the criteria for selection. A coach also needs to connect to parents and justify their family member's participation in esports, especially if recruiting is a part of the role. A sample position description for the role of coach is shown in Figure 2.2.

Find the Right Faculty
Recruitment and selection of faculty for curricular elements of an esports program at a college or university will vary by the discipline with which the content will be associated and the type of institution at which the program is being developed. No matter the field or the college or university, a number of considerations are common in hiring new faculty. The ability to teach well, a record of scholarship (research, publications, and presentations) or evidence of the likelihood to actively engage in scholarly endeavors, experience in mentoring graduate students, and a collegial approach to engaging as a member of a department and an institution are among the factors typically evaluated. One other, which is common in research institutions, is a record of attracting external funding or evidence of the ability to attract external funding to support a research agenda. When it comes to faculty involved in esports programming, this ability to attract funding may involve support for research. It may, however, also be about the ability to work with institutional development staff and others to attract support in the form of gifts or sponsorships to help fund the program itself.

Figure 2.2. Sample position description for an esports coach.

> Reporting to the director of student activities, the esports coach must provide strategic leadership for the esports program while supporting the wider mission and goals of the college. The coach is responsible for all aspects of coaching the esports team including recruiting, training, supervision, and coaching at practices, competitions, and regular meetings with the esports team. The coach will advocate for the importance of an esports program within the campus community, as well as the larger community, and will serve as a role model of the high standards expected of our students. A successful candidate will have experience recruiting students, as well as cultivating friends of the various programs to meet enrollment and fundraising goals. The successful candidate should demonstrate and support a commitment and sensitivity to diversity, gender equity, and equal opportunity.
>
> Essential Functions
>
> - Use the college's mission and strategic plan as a guideline to develop and direct the esports program.
> - Ensure an environment that promotes student safety.
> - Work with director of student activities to monitor progress and eligibility of all students.
> - Work with director of student activities and admissions staff to establish annual recruitment goals.
> - Serve on various campus committees as appointed by the dean of students.
> - Cultivate positive relationships with students and their families.
> - Develop a positive relationship with and play an active role in college and community events and programs.
> - Work collaboratively with student services and residence life staff with respect to student needs and any issues related to student behavior.

(Continues)

Figure 2.2. (*Continued*)

- Ensure institutional compliance with the various governing bodies for the esports program.
- Collaborate with the director of student activities in establishing a fundraising plan for esports programs that meets the department's annual fundraising goals and aligns with the college's overall fundraising strategy.
- Prepare an annual budget for the esports program.
- Develop practice schedules and a training program as appropriate.
- Coordinate with the director of student activities to integrate the esports team into the current recreational esports program and provide support to the larger gaming community on campus.
- Coordinate with the athletic conference to establish a collegiate-level program within the conference.
- Ensure the highest ethical, moral, and spiritual standards for all aspects of the program.
- Promote and manage a summer camp program in coordination with auxiliary services and athletics that helps achieve the fundraising goals of the department.

Creating a Successful and Inclusive Cocurricular Model for Esports

Esports has the potential to be one of the most inclusive cocurricular programs on a campus, but often these programs can be male dominated and with this a number of problems can arise if we are not intentional in our design. Chapter 5 examines in detail issues of sexism, racism, and homophobia that can occur in esports and emphasizes the importance of building an inclusive model. For the purpose of this section we are not minimizing the need to focus on inclusivity in curricular esports programming but rather recognizing that those efforts will relate to matters of pedagogy for which others are better positioned to offer detailed advice. Neither are we seeking to minimize the importance of inclusivity from a social justice lens, but we are simply focused on a broader view, which would also include desired levels of competition (competitive versus recreational) and diversity in games played and formats of games played.

You should have a solid inventory of who is playing what games in what format on your campus as a starting point for considering developing inclusive cocurricular esports programming. It will be important to bring together as many of your current students involved in esports as possible and begin to form a common set of goals aimed at forming an inclusive organization to help them thrive. This seems like a great deal of effort, but we caution against skipping this step. One college started a sponsored varsity esports team that lost to another team from that same college in a competition, and it caused several issues as the student-athletes rebelled against what they saw as an administration attempting to control them. To avoid this mistake, approach this process with an open mind. Start by determining what you as the college can bring to the table and on what level and in what areas the students can have ownership.

Offer a Varsity and Club Program

Our belief is that creating opportunities to participate in esports at various levels of competition maximizes the potential to meet recruitment and retention goals through esports programming. You may find that students gravitate to one or the other of these opportunities, and it may be that some students will be involved in both if institutional policies and competition schedules permit.

You may consider creating a varsity team with a list of approved games and an established season and competition schedule. This roster is selected and directly controlled by the esports coach. In addition to the varsity roster you should establish a club that is open to all students and offers a path to become a varsity member. The club can be advised by the coach, but it should be led by the students. Remember, they need to own it.

It should not be difficult to draw the line between the team and the club. A varsity team should meet the standards of any other similar program. It would have a practice schedule as well as study halls, with times established by the coach. Team members would have travel costs covered and would receive uniforms just like any other team on campus. They would also be required to meet minimum academic standards and participate in competitions.

The club members would have more say in how they participate. For instance, they may only meet once a month and would compete only in local events. Students who are not a part of the varsity team may simply want to play a game because they love it, and the competitive nature, in the tournament sense, does not serve their interests. With the structure of a student club providing students the power to self-select their preferences of membership, you are still creating a gaming environment and you are opening that experience to a wider audience.

This model will also allow a program to offer more than just the most standard or current games as options for students. One school has a Magic the Gathering/Dungeons & Dragons tabletop group that is a part of their program and has opened up membership to students who participate in gaming more as a matter of social engagement or a hobby than as a form of competition and performance. In this model a college esports program can offer a larger variety of games. This will allow flexibility as games lose or gain popularity. An esports program designed in this way can adapt as these changes occur—and they inevitably will.

Learning Outcomes for Esports Programs

Another very important part of the building process for a new esports program is establishing learning outcomes. This is a routine part of pedagogical practice in curricular programs, so we will focus our comments in this section on developing learning outcomes for cocurricular elements of an esports program. Sadly, this process is sometimes overlooked in professional practice. However, for a cocurricular esports program to be successful in the long run, it will need to demonstrate that it contributes to the academic mission of the college. Articulating learning outcomes (we include student development and learning in this phrasing) early in the development of a cocurricular esports program will prove invaluable later, in terms of both assessment and justifying the continued existence of the program.

As an initial step, we encourage readers to consider reviewing any institution-level learning outcomes or general education outcomes articulated by the faculty. Connecting program-level learning outcomes for esports to these established outcomes, where they exist, is good practice in that it supports the linkage between the curriculum and cocurriculum. It is also politically savvy in that it can foster support among faculty for the cocurricular elements of an institutional esports effort (Barr et al., 2014). When it comes to developing those program-level learning outcomes, it can be helpful to engage faculty colleagues experienced in developing learning outcomes to serve as consultants for the work.

A learning outcome is simply a statement of what a participant should and will learn as a result of participation in your program. Bloom's taxonomy (Bloom et al., 1956) can provide a useful framework around which to structure learning outcomes that reflect increasing levels of cognitive complexity. The taxonomy and examples of verbs associated with the various levels of learning are shared in the following:

- *Remembering:* define, list, recognize
- *Understanding:* characterize, describe, explain, identify, locate, recognize, sort

- *Applying:* choose, demonstrate, implement, perform
- *Analyzing:* analyze, categorize, compare, differentiate
- *Evaluating:* assess, critique, evaluate, rank, rate
- *Synthesizing/creating:* construct, design, formulate, organize, synthesize

The example in Figure 2.3 from a fictitious college may assist you in thinking critically about learning outcome development and the relationship among mission, strategic goals, divisional priorities, learning outcomes and assessment.

After you have developed outcomes, you should spend time considering what strategies you will implement to help achieve these outcomes. Having these written out will help guide you as you design the day-to-day operations of the program. Figure 2.3 shows a set of strategies connected to the learning outcomes at XYZ College.

- Coach and student relationships
- Individual team meetings regarding policies and procedures, eligibility, and so on
- Midterm grade process
- Community service projects
- Student advisory program
- Collaboration with student conduct office
- Mandatory training and Title IX program

Once you have the outcomes and have developed strategies to address them, you will need to find a way to measure if you have achieved these or not by developing an assessment plan. Assessment plans are specific ways progress can be measured to determine if a program is achieving its learning outcomes. The following list describes examples of assessment tools that can be used to measure progress toward the established learning outcomes at XYZ College:

- Student GPA
- Fall survey
- Conduct reports
- End-of-season survey
- Graduation rates and retention rates
- Progress reports for individual students

Figure 2.3. Sample of learning outcomes for a cocurricular esports program.

> XYZ College is a place of opportunity. We offer undergraduate and graduate students a personalized, integrated, and holistic educational experience that prepares them for meaningful work and purposeful lives in a changing global society. Students study in depth in a specific area of interest while acquiring broad skills and habits of mind to navigate a complex, diverse, and unscripted future.
>
> Esports at XYZ contributes to the holistic learning environment by providing and cultivating specific skills that will benefit students long after graduation. Students who take part in cocurricular esports programs at XYZ will be able to
>
> - Form positive relationships with faculty, staff, and students
> - Describe and demonstrate healthy habits in relation to alcohol/substances, nutrition, stress, fitness, relationships, conflict resolution, hazing prevention, and so on
> - Apply interpersonal skills that increase their ability to work with others, effectively communicate, and develop supportive teammate relationships
> - Demonstrate an understanding of policies, procedures, and expectations of XYZ College and the esports program
> - Recognize and choose to participate in opportunities for community service, civic engagement, and leadership
> - Demonstrate integration into the campus culture and educational mission by academic success and persistence to graduation

Building an Esports Arena

Considering facilities is also an important part of developing an esports program on campus. The facilities required for curricular elements of an esports program will vary depending on the discipline and the nature of the academic program. The requirements for a course on digital marketing are different from those for a course on game design. Given this variability, we will focus this section on facilities to support cocurricular esports programming.

The facilities you will need depend on the scale and scope of the cocurricular esports program you have in mind. The basic requirements are a computer lab for practice, suitable to the size of the team you intend to support and types of games in which you intend to compete, along with an office for the adviser or coach. Moving across the continuum of ambition and complexity, one could imagine a practice space, a competition space with seating for an audience and large monitors to view the team as it participates, a space to support digital streaming, and offices for a coach and staff involved in supporting the team. The advice we offer in the following paragraphs is intended to be helpful no matter where a particular college or university falls along that continuum.

Balancing Aspirations and Resources
The first step in considering facilities needs for a cocurricular esports program is to consider what type of program your institution hopes to develop. As a matter of general advice, we encourage three strategies in this consideration. First, we encourage readers to plan for success. This is not to say build for a fanciful overestimation of potential, but try to build a bit more than you think you may need so that you have the room for the program to grow in the future. Second, think in stages. It may not be necessary, or even possible, to repurpose or build everything you want in a single project. Give thought to how portions of the overall facilities plan might be sequenced. Third, we turn to Barr and McClellan's (2018) discussion of planning for such projects. They began by identifying the dilemma that confronts many who have engaged in facilities design.

> Groups involved in the planning of a capital project often find themselves in a "chicken and egg" scenario. . . . Should they plan for what they can afford, or should they seek to fund what they plan? The former may limit the possibilities of the project; the latter may lead to delays in initiating the project pending securing of funds or to complications late in the project when cuts in the plan have to be made quickly because the necessary funding fails to materialize. (p. 138)

They went on to propose a way to approach planning that may help in addressing the problem as described.

> One strategy for addressing the dilemma . . . is to begin by pursuing a process of what the Walt Disney Company refers to as *Imagineering*. In considering new projects, the Disney team begins project development by imagining what they would like the project to be and then considering how that imaginative vision might be engineered. (p. 138)

Imagineering encourages planning for what is desirable and then pursuing how to make it possible, as opposed to beginning the planning process by defining limits or constraints. Combining Imagineering with Mills's (2003) notion of value engineering has real promise for facilities planning in higher education. Barr and McClellan (2018) described value engineering as

> a collaborative effort of representatives from the institution as well as firms involved in the design, development, and construction of the project, with the goal of that effort being to make informed decisions regarding features of the project that will allow the greatest realization of the imagined possibility while adhering to the practical reality of the budget available. (p. 138)

Identifying the Space
Most colleges and universities beginning an esports program are more likely to repurpose and adapt extant space rather than build new space. Start by taking an inventory of all the spaces you have on campus that could serve as a home for your cocurricular esports programs (curricular spaces vary so widely that detailed discussion is impractical). An ideal setup would include 14 computer gaming stations and a small area for lounging. You should look for a space between 800 and 1,000 square feet as a starting point.

Consider how you want the esports space used as you build your program. If you are including both a club and varsity program, you may need times that the space is restricted to varsity members for practice. You might include a console gaming area if you have the space. A PC lab will meet most of your esports needs, but many games are only available on a console offered by companies like Nintendo, Sony, or Microsoft. There is some thought that console gaming is a part of esports that is more inclusive for people from minoritized groups (see chapter 5). You may also want to designate times the space is open to all students so you further encourage gaming on campus. Be sure you have a way to monitor usage so you can report that in your assessment.

Give thought to a streaming area for students to stream games and provide commentary during your matches. This is an entire subindustry of esports that has exploded. You may also want to plan for live audiences to watch competitions. This would require additional space for theater-style seating as well as large video displays to observe the action.

It is likely that student recruitment will be one of the goals your institution has in implementing an esports program. Think about having the space in a highly trafficked area of campus so that it can be shown off as part of campus tours and so that it can more easily accommodate spectators if you plan to include that in your program.

Another thing to keep in mind in regard to the location of the space is that you may want to grant after-hours access to students so they may take advantage of the space. This could be done by having coded door access or through a key card system. It is not a requirement, but students will expect this at some point.

Power and internet connectivity are critical, so make sure you involve your facilities and IT staff in the discussion of possibilities. Also note that these spaces can get very warm, as people and equipment will both generate heat. You will need to identify a space that can be kept cool. Finally, windows are not a bad idea, but make sure you have a way to make the room as dark as possible during the day.

Developing the Space
Once you have identified the space, you will need to prep the space by designing the layout and making sure all cables for connectivity and electric supply are run. The design should keep in mind that you will have, at any one time, two teams competing. A great idea would be to have half the stations at one end of the space and the other half at the opposite end, with lounge space in the middle. This will help minimize cross-talk during practice and competitions.

Outfitting the Space
The next step is to purchase furniture and equipment to outfit the space. If done correctly, plan to spend around $35,000 to $50,000 to equip the space with gaming stations and peripherals. You can find great deals on computers, desks, and gaming chairs at a cost of about $2,000 per setup. Here again, you will have additional expenses associated with including an area for live spectators. You will also have expenses to include the capacity for streaming your competitions.

The safety and security of players, coaches, and spectators must be a part of designing and planning for an esports facility on campus. The esports space should be covered either by live monitoring or video monitoring as much as possible. A simple check-in station with a laptop equipped with a card reader and software that connects security cameras to campus security or another monitoring service are important.

Comfortable Space
The last step is to make your space look and feel like a place students would want to come to play esports. The facility should not appear to be simply another computer lab on campus. Have the students discuss ways to design and decorate the space so it meets their needs and has both a functional and "cool" feel to it.

Conclusion

Esports is growing rapidly on college campuses. This chapter offers broad advice intended to help you on a path to planning successful curricular and cocurricular programming for your college or university, but you will need to design a program that fits your student body and your campus culture.

As you seek input from others, make sure you are hearing all voices. Esports offers an opportunity to engage students from all areas on campus, but this must be an intentional and deliberate effort. Esports can be an overwhelmingly male-dominated sport and often the atmosphere created can be less than inclusive (see chapter 5). Programs should constantly question this and look for ways to include all students in their programs. This can be accomplished through targeted recruitment and inclusion efforts.

The creation of an esports program is not a small undertaking, but it can be accomplished and can be scaled up or down to fit your campus. The more planning and preparation that is accomplished prior to a launch, the smoother it will go, but be prepared for bumps and roadblocks along the way. Facilities issues, leadership changes, technology struggles, and even shipping delays can cause headaches.

The best advice that can be offered is that you do not have to know everything. You are not alone. There are quite a few people out in the world looking at building solid programs who are in the same boat, along with a good number who have already done it. Ask questions and get help when you can. Having an outside person visit your campus and work with your team to get you started could prove invaluable if you are lost and could also save you thousands of dollars in time and money.

We close this chapter with a final bit of advice. The success of your program will be directly impacted by the people involved. They will be far more critical than the technology, space, and peripherals. Spend most of your time designing the program with this in mind.

3

RUNNING A COCURRICULAR ESPORTS PROGRAM

The previous chapter presented information and advice on getting an esports program started on campus. This chapter focuses on running an esports program once it is established; that is, addressing the ongoing management of cocurricular programming, as we believe there are interesting and unique aspects to it about which we may be able to provide helpful insight and encouragement. This is not to detract from the importance of providing leadership for ongoing curricular esports offerings. The continuing management of curricular esports programming is akin to the ongoing administration of any academic program. Most decisions are local to the faculty member and department colleagues directly engaged in the academic activity, and the variables associated with those decisions vary widely across the type of activity (e.g., short course, symposium, or full course), academic discipline, and type of institution. We will simply note here that there is a need in the scholarship of teaching and learning and the scholarship of practice for publications focused on esports in the curriculum.

Managing a successful cocurricular esports program can be a daunting task for a number of reasons. Our goal in this chapter will be to provide concrete suggestions that will help a college or university to efficiently and effectively manage a student esports organization or team. Although no one model will be ideal for all colleges, we believe that, as a result of sharing experiences and lessons learned in managing esports, a college esports adviser or coach may be able to avoid some mistakes and have a program that helps a college meet its institutional mission.

The chapter opens with an exploration of the multiple roles that the staff leader of a cocurricular esports program, whether group adviser or team coach, needs to fulfill in order for the program to be successful. Then the chapter will attempt to shed light on ways a college can manage and run an esports program that serves a number of purposes and contributes to the learning environment. The discussion will highlight four aspects of managing cocurricular esports: the structure of the program, competition and the various avenues by which a college can choose to compete, management of an esports arena, and the importance of the adviser or coach. We will center the experiences of one particular institution as an example of an institution working its way through each of these four aspects of esports program management.

Roles of an Esports Staff Leader

Once an esports organization or team is up and running, the work of the staff becomes complex and multifaceted. That work includes the obvious and important administrative tasks associated with managing any university program, but it also includes the arguably more important activity of interactions with students and student-athletes.

Students today are forcing us to rethink how we meet our obligations to them. We are seeing a shift in demand from amenities to services, and today's students are far more money conscious than the previous generation (Selingo, 2018). They also see getting a job as the primary reason to attend college. They have been described as loyal, needy (emotionally), thoughtful, open-minded, responsible (crave order and predictability), and determined (Seemiller & Grace, 2015). Technology has become an indispensable part of this generation's lives, more than any other generation to date, and as a result they may need more in the way of social and emotional support than previous generations (Selingo, 2018). A structured and functioning esports program can help meet this need, and staff (staff members or faculty acting as student organization advisers or team coaches) in those programs may serve as coaches, advisers, counselors, and educators for students.

Coaching

The coaching role (both the informal coaching done by an adviser of a registered student organization and the formal coaching done by staff for club or varsity teams) includes oversight of recruiting and training, attention to health and safety issues, management of practice and competition schedules, and assurance of compliance with the rules and policies of the institution related to club or varsity sports as well as any rules and policies of relevant associations, conferences, or leagues in which the team competes. This is the most obvious of the roles a staff member involved in esports will play. Coaches are typically hired based on their experience in coaching or participation in the sport or activity. Yet, as we pointed out in chapter 2, success in coaching and managing a program will be based in significant part on a coach's ability to manage the student experience beyond gaming.

Advising

The staff of a cocurricular esports program might also be expected to manage academic success outcomes for students. Both student organization advisers and team coaches are called upon to ensure that students taking part in their programs are eligible to do so. Chambliss (2014) made an argument that face-to-face interaction is more important now than ever before and creating personal connections between a student and a faculty or staff member can have a positive impact on retention and academic success. Coaches, particularly coaches with whom students develop important relationships, may also be asked for advice on courses or careers. A coach who is doing their job well and creating a positive environment will begin to mentor students in a variety of ways.

Counseling

Steven Mintz (2019) stated colleges have a

> responsibility to educate the whole person, promote students' social, emotional, and interpersonal development and embrace Arthur Chickering's call for institutions to help students define an adult identity, learn to manage their emotions, develop mature interpersonal relationships, and chart clear vocational goals. (para. 18)

As counselors, esports coaches need to be prepared to support the whole student experience. This role will be the most difficult challenge that any coach or adviser of a program will face, and colleges often do not do enough to provide professional development in helping new staff cultivate the required skills to help students as they navigate this transitional time in their lives.

Educating

George Kuh (1996) is among those who have pointed out the importance of purposeful and thoughtful linkages between curricular and cocurricular learning. Barr et al. (2014) made the argument that folks in student affairs (and, for that matter, folks in athletics) have a role to play as educators. Several times in these early chapters, we have pointed out the importance of connecting esports programming at a college or university to the academic mission of that institution. Advisers and coaches of cocurricular esports organizations or teams must think of one of their roles as being that of educator in order for a program to be truly successful in this regard.

Having a clear sense of what good teaching and learning looks like will be integral to how well a staff member fulfills their role as educator. Barr et al. (2014) pointed to a set of 10 principles articulated in *Powerful Partnerships: A Shared Responsibility for Learning* (American Association for Higher Education et al., 1998) as a helpful guide. They summarized those principles as the following:

1. Learning is fundamentally about making and maintaining connections: biologically through neural networks; mentally among concepts, ideas, and meanings; and experientially through interaction between the mind and the environment, self and other, generality and context, deliberation and action.
2. Learning is enhanced by taking place in the context of a compelling situation that balances challenge and opportunity, stimulating and utilizing the brain's ability to conceptualize quickly and its capacity and need for contemplation and reflection upon experiences.
3. Learning is an active search for meaning by the learner—constructing knowledge rather than passively receiving it, shaping as well as being shaped by experiences.
4. Learning is developmental, a cumulative process involving the whole person, relating past and present, integrating the new with the old, starting from but transcending personal concerns and interests.
5. Learning is done by individuals who are intrinsically tied to others as social beings, interacting as competitors or collaborators, constraining or supporting the learning process, and able to enhance learning through cooperation and sharing.
6. Learning is strongly affected by the educational climate in which it takes place: the settings and surroundings, the influences of others, and the values accorded to the life of the mind and to learning achievements.
7. Learning requires frequent feedback if it is to be sustained, practice if it is to be nourished, and opportunities to use what has been learned.

8. Much learning takes place informally and incidentally, beyond explicit teaching or the classroom, in casual contacts with faculty and staff, peers, campus life, active social and community involvements, and unplanned but fertile and complex situations.
9. Learning is grounded in particular contexts and individual experiences, requiring effort to transfer specific knowledge and skills to other circumstances or to more general understandings and to unlearn personal views and approaches when confronted by new information.
10. Learning involves the ability of individuals to monitor their own learning, to understand how knowledge is acquired, to develop strategies for learning based on discerning their capacities and limitations, and to be aware of their own ways of knowing in approaching new bodies of knowledge and disciplinary frameworks. (Barr et al., 2014, pp. 137–139)

One can easily see how readily the esports environment lends itself to the application of these principles and likely affords a multitude of teachable moments (Havighurst, 1952). Staff members who see themselves as educators and ensure that learning outcomes are articulated for the program, prepare themselves with pedagogical strategies to foster student learning, and scan for those moments of opportunity will be tremendous assets to their students, their program, and their institution.

Employing Esports Coaches

Hiring and retaining a good coach are critical to sustain a successful cocurricular esports program. This chapter describes the multiple roles that a coach plays, building on chapter 2's description of some of the challenges for a college or university in hiring a coach with college-level experience or with professional experience in gaming. Finding one person who can fulfill robust expectations in regard to supporting students; administering the program; ensuring health, safety, and compliance; and helping cultivate resources to support the program is going to be difficult. This section suggests how institutions can meet the coaching needs for their esports program.

We begin the discussion by making what we hope will be a helpful comparison. Typical coaching hires are for a single sport such as football, soccer, or volleyball. They may even be for a particular aspect of a single sport, such as an offensive line coach. This is not the case with esports programs in which the intention is to compete in more than one game. Here colleges and universities are usually hiring one coach to provide support for student-athletes competing in all esports games. Sometimes they are competing across different platforms such as computer or console. The coach may also be providing support for a recognized student organization and a club team. With the exception of the latter elements, the closest parallel for most institutions is in track and field or gymnastics. They have athletes competing in multiple events. In the case of track and field, athletes compete both indoors and outdoors. A track coach or gymnastics coach may have a basic understanding of all the events and even be considered proficient in one or two events. Very few, if any, coaches would have the expertise needed to guide and coach all of these events at a level that could benefit a college participant. A shotput coach would not automatically make a great pole-vaulting coach. Similarly, an esports coach who has expertise in League of Legends may know little or nothing about Smash Brothers. This presents a challenge for esports that can be easily solved in much the same way college track teams do, by hiring consultant coaches to help support the work of your primary coach.

The great thing about esports is that these consulting coaches can help virtually and need not be on-site. This could save a great deal of money and really help move a team forward. There are hundreds (if not thousands) of coaches out there for esports, charging rates between $10/hour and $100/hour. These coaches can be found a number of ways. Sites like Gamer Sensei offer a platform that connects coaches from a variety of games to players around the world. A suggested approach is to identify a consultant coach, have a trial period for a few practice sessions, and see if the chemistry is right and if the players feel the relationship will benefit them. The great thing about this model is that you are not obligated to keep a coach who does not fit. Once you find a coach you like, you should move to a monthly rate and even set up an understanding that the coach remain throughout an entire season. In this case the coach will be more committed to the team and will be able to build a better understanding of the team dynamics and player tendencies that can only be developed in long-term coaching arrangements. Of course, in an ideal world, having a coach who can be present physically is the best option, but budget and expertise will inevitably drive these decisions.

Creating Structure Within a Program: The Case of Schreiner University

Chapter 2 discussed the importance of encouraging students to take a significant role in leading esports programming and examined the benefits of building a program that from the beginning has student buy-in and input. It also examined the benefit of creating a structure that allows for competitive and recreational players to be involved. This section of the chapter will describe, as a type of short case study, one school's attempt to follow through on such a structure and will provide lessons learned as that university has navigated this landscape. In the spirit of full disclosure, one of this book's coauthors was an active participant in the creation of the program at that institution and continues to be involved in ongoing oversight for that program.

In 2016 Schreiner University (SU), a small liberal arts university in Kerrville, Texas, ambitiously set out to create an esports program. It began to invest money and launched the program fully in the fall of 2018 after a year of planning. The university's founding principle was one of inclusion, and early on it made a commitment that any student could find a home on the esports team. The program contains both a varsity team and a club team to help encourage involvement. The varsity team is coached by a full-time esports coach who reports to the director of student activities, and the club is managed by the students and advised by the esports coach.

Varsity Team

The varsity team is specifically recruited and is designed to be the competitive branch of the esports program. SU views the varsity esports program like any other athletic program, including established GPA requirements.

Expectations of Players

The coach, who organizes mandatory study halls and prescribed practice times, has set forth the following expectations in a comprehensive handbook for esports players:

- Players are expected to maintain a team-first mentality at all times. This includes not acting above any other team member and striving to improve together as a team. Failure to do so may result in a warning if the coach feels a player is not exhibiting this mentality.
- Players should always exhibit a desire to not only improve as individuals but also with a focus on how that improvement will impact the team as a whole.
- Players are expected to be able to provide and receive criticism as it relates to their team and game. Criticism that is not deemed as constructive will not be allowed (i.e., telling someone they are bad).
- Players must be able to listen to their teammates' criticism without feeling personally attacked. There should be productive discussion and not excessive arguing.
- Players are expected to come to practice, matches, and events with a positive attitude.

- Poor attitude such as not communicating, communicating negatively, or behaving in a toxic manner will require a meeting with the coach, and further action may be taken such as warnings or a suspension.
- This is considered a professional environment and will be treated as such. Cursing will not be allowed. Cursing may result in a warning at the discretion of the coach.
- Harassment of any kind will not be tolerated at all. Depending on severity, harassment of any kind will result in a warning or even immediate suspension. Anything deemed as extreme harassment may result in removal from the team or program. Additionally, any form of harassment will need to be reported to the university for review. (Lucich & Gehrels, 2019, pp. 13–14)

Chapter 5 discusses in depth a number of these issues and other concerns associated with college esports so we will not explore them in depth here. Simply note at this point that it is important to have an understanding of these issues in operating an ongoing program. Outlining player behavior expectations from the outset can help establish a positive culture from the beginning.

Game and Player Selection
The coach determines on an annual basis which games will be offered (within the parameters of any discussion by the institution of alignment of values and games in which the school will compete) and establishes a selection criterion for players to compete in each game. Choosing which games your esports program will compete in is not an overly complicated task, but it is an important one. You must look at what opportunities for competition exist and the skill your players (current or recruits) bring to the team. SU's varsity esports program chose to focus on League of Legends, Overwatch, Smash Brothers, and Rocket League as the primary competitive games for the 2019–2020 competition season.

Setting Roster and Schedules for Practice and Competition
The coach completes three tasks once the games are identified: establishes who competes in each of these games, creates a practice schedule to maximize the use of space, and builds a competition schedule that provides the right balance of challenge and success (more on this later in the chapter).

One way to establish the competition teams for each game is to host a regular playoff that creates a ranking system and in which players compete for roster spots. Another way is to simply have the coach make the decision. Competing for a roster spot on a weekly basis may provide a competitive team environment that strengthens the skills of the team, but it could also divide the team. In addition, sometimes players perform well in the familiar environment of in-house competition but fail to perform at the same level in actual competition. Having the coach manage competition can mitigate the chances of the team becoming overly competitive, but this team competition may also create an illusion of favoritism. These questions are simple when talking about one-on-one games and competition selection method is the obvious answer. It is not so simple in the team-based games like League of Legends and Overwatch. A coach should know their own team well enough to know what will work and what may not.

Once the team has an established procedure for roster selection, the coach will need to create a practice schedule. The most important and seemingly most obvious step is to understand the students' class schedules. Participants in college sports are student-athletes, and the student part will always need to come first. This philosophy should be established early in any program. By creating a master calendar that has the students' class schedules, a coach can gain a better understanding of what time slots are available for practice. Establishing a practice structure will also be dependent on the availability of space, the size and setup of that space, and sometimes the location of the space (if you have to practice off campus).

A college may want to consider a rotating practice schedule where the teams can have exclusive access to the space while they practice. League of Legends and Overwatch practices, for example, will involve a great deal of discussion. Having a Smash Brothers practice in the same space could get pretty loud and would be a distraction to both groups. College and university esports programs will benefit from offering open play times in their space, but the varsity student-athletes will need time to focus. Designated practices will help facilitate this.

The last task the coach will need to accomplish is creating a competition structure. This will be addressed in great detail in a later section, but flexibility and creativity are keys to having a meaningful competition structure.

Club Team

The second and larger part of SU's esports program is the club program. Named the Gamers' Guild, the club is really intended to open the door of esports for all students who show an interest. The group's constitution, which it calls a creed, is shown in Appendix 3A.

The club is managed under a student leadership model and is connected to the esports team as the club's adviser is also the varsity esports coach. The two teams share a game facility. The varsity team has priority on practice times, but the club has access to the space and will scrimmage with the varsity team.

Game Selection
The students taking part in the guild select the games in which it participates. Any institution, particularly a public institution, would be well advised to steer clear of any attempt to prohibit a club program or recognized student organization from playing a particular title or type of game, though an institution could encourage the student leadership to consider values alignment as part of their selection.

Governance
The emphasis in a club team is on student leaders. There are a number of elected officers whose portfolio includes the entire club team. These include president, secretary, treasurer, and public relations officer. The club team has three divisions: computer, console, and hobby games. Each of the three game divisions in the club program is represented by a vice president. These seven student officers and the club esports coach make up the executive council for the guild.

Like student organizations on campuses across the country, the guild has a constitution that lays out its structure and governance processes. That document is shared at the end of this chapter.

Communication

A program designed with a dual structure like SU's faces challenges in balancing the needs of both groups and creating opportunities for meaningful participation for all members of both the varsity team and club members. SU utilizes a communication tool called Discord to aid in managing this complex structure. Discord is a free-to-use communication application that has more advanced features than professional applications like Microsoft Teams, Cisco Jabber, and Slack. Discord also has a robust mobile client built in.

The software allows for general communication channels as well as specific channels students can self-sort themselves into. Discord allows for locked channels that can include adviser chats, executive chats, and sponsor chats so that business can be handled when participants are not able to meet in person. SU has open chats set up for each division of the guild with a separate chat for each game that falls under that division. The varsity teams also have their own chat channels. For example, there are two Overwatch chats—one for students on the varsity team and one for the club. It falls underneath PC and console gaming, so it has its own server. This allows practice times, team meetings, and so on to be listed for those on the varsity team, while allowing club players to still talk about the game or set up times to play with other gamers.

We highlight the SU model in this section as it offers a view of options for teams that aligns with our discussion in chapter 2. A college program could start with a club team and transition into a varsity program, and each of those options would require a slightly different structure in terms of practice times and competition schedules.

Creating a Competition Structure

Another important part of managing an ongoing cocurricular esports program is creating and sustaining a meaningful competition schedule. Esports has two factors that separate it out from other college sports programs when it comes to scheduling. First, esports competition does not necessarily require travel, though some travel ought to be a part of the student-athlete experience (see chapter 2). Second, esports does not have a set competition structure that mirrors the NCAA or other large sports sanctioning bodies (see chapter 1). Both of these circumstances present challenges and opportunities when it comes to competition structure. A program coach will need to be diligent in establishing competition. Finding solid competition, sorting through all of the competing opportunities, and monitoring the rapidly developing competition landscape is one of the most challenging things a coach will face.

Something to consider when developing and sustaining a competition structure for a college or university cocurricular esports program is assessing which of the available options and opportunities might best suit the needs of your program. Associations like NACE and Tespa offer connections to the college esports world, and leagues like CSL and SLICE are establishing themselves as competitive environments for college teams. Some NCAA conferences like the Peach Belt Conference and the Southern Collegiate Athletic Conference have established competitions for their member schools and offer an annual conference championship. There are even opportunities through some of the more popular games like League of Legends, which offers its own college competition structure called College LoL.

From joining an association or a league to creating a league with your existing athletic conference or even connecting with individual schools to create a custom competition experience, a number of logistical complications will inevitably pop up. Any seasoned coach for any sport or program will tell you the first year is by far the most challenging. As you build a network of colleagues and create connections you will find that creating a schedule is possible. Prepare yourself for the idea that the first year may not look exactly as you imagined.

A program that is getting started in this process should consider finding a built-in competition schedule if possible, in an established league such as CSL or SLICE. The primary deciding factors on league or association should be which games they offer and the cost associated with joining. Another factor to consider is the competition level. Some leagues will have more established teams from larger programs, and entering these leagues may be similar to a small independent NCAA Division III college facing a Division I powerhouse in football or basketball. A program should look for competition that offers the best balance between an opportunity to win and enough challenge to improve. Many programs belong to multiple leagues and have found varying degrees of success in each.

Managing an Esports Arena

One of the single best investments in terms of dollars is the creation of an attractive and functional space for your esports program. Chapter 2 points to the associated costs and provides a few tips on how a college could organize an esports arena or lab. Here we will briefly discuss the management of that space and some of the challenges a coach may face in this process.

An esports team is not unlike a basketball, soccer, or volleyball program in some ways. They all need a space to practice and sharpen their skills. Esports teams also need specialized equipment to function, and this means computers, peripherals, and servers, so security is a priority. An ideal space for esports has adequate security camera coverage and access to the space is controlled. If possible, card swipe access should be considered, which allows students to have controlled access to the space. Most card access systems will allow the administrator to limit access by card number (student ID) and by date and time. For instance, you could limit the team captain for Overwatch to only access the space with their card on Mondays, Wednesdays, and Fridays from 3:00 pm to 6:00 pm. This would require a few details to set up and would also be dependent on the capabilities of the system. Coaches should reach out to their technology department to determine the full capabilities of a card system to take full advantage of it. You can look at a key box or coded door lock if a card system is not possible or too cost prohibitive, but these may be less secure and do not have a log that tracks use. The last option is to ensure that your coach or a staff member is always present when the space is used. That can prove to be difficult as a program grows and if you hope to maximize the use of that space.

Table 3.1 shows a sample arena schedule for an esports program with five competitive teams in Smash Brothers, Rocket League, Overwatch, League of Legends, and PlayerUnknown's Battlegrounds. It also provides for open play and a weekly team meeting.

This sample arena would be used 72 hours a week even being closed on Sundays. It would be difficult to manage this space without student leadership even if there were two staff members assigned to the program, especially if you expected your coach(es) to attend staff meetings, teach a course, serve on committees, recruit new student-athletes, handle administrative tasks and meetings, and help with fundraising. Scheduling the space will depend on the availability of students and will need to consider the students' course schedules. You do not see the team's study hall hours on this schedule; those could and should occur in another space on campus.

TABLE 3.1
Sample Schedule for Esports Arena

Time	Mon	Tues	Weds	Thurs	Fri	Sat	Sun
10:00 a.m.	OP	OP	OP	OP	OP		
11:00 a.m.	OP	OP	OP	OP	OP		
12:00 p.m.	OP	OP	OP	OP	OP		
1:00 p.m.	SB	RL	SB	RL	SB	OP	
2:00 p.m.	SB	RL	SB	RL	SB	OP	
3:00 p.m.	LoL	OW	LoL	OW	LoL	OP	
4:00 p.m.	LoL	OW	LoL	OW	LoL	OP	
5:00 p.m.	LoL	OW	LoL	OW	LoL	OP	
6:00 p.m.	OP	PUBG	OP	PUBG	OP	LoL	
7:00 p.m.	OP	PUBG	OP	PUBG	OP	LoL	
8:00 p.m.	OW	LoL		TM	OW	LoL	
9:00 p.m.	OW	LoL		TM	OW	OW	
10:00 p.m.	OW	LoL		TM	OW	OW	

Note. LoL = League of Legends; OP = Open play; OW = Overwatch; PUBG = PlayerUnknown's Battlegrounds; SB = Super Smash Bros.; TM = Team meeting; RL = Rocket League.

Student schedules should be a consideration when scheduling the esports arena, with an eye toward helping students balance the amount of time they need to practice and want to practice. It will not be uncommon for students to spend entirely too much time in the space, and if grades start to slip that can be an issue (see chapter 4 for insights into the experiences of an esports athlete and issues of time management and academic performance). As a rule, athletes should spend no more than 3 to 4 hours a day on practice. A program may want to create a practice log to help monitor this. Where the challenge will occur is if students choose to participate on their own time. Coaches should address this at the beginning of each season and really work to help students understand the importance of rest and diet on performance.

One final point in regard to managing an esports arena. Coaches should consider limiting the use of food and beverages in the space. We would suggest not allowing food or drink at the game stations and instead creating a break area in the space for snacks and drinks. A space that is used more than 72 hours a week by more than 50 students who are constantly coming and going will need to be cleaned regularly. Create a daily and weekly to-do list that ensures the space is presentable. A space should also be deep cleaned once a month, including complete dusting of all equipment and peripherals.

A dedicated space for an esports program will in many ways serve as a living room for the team. It can be a place where students practice and spend social time. Research for years has shown that students who socially connect with one another are more successful in terms of academic performance, retention, and graduation (Mayhew et al., 2016). Creating and properly managing a space for esports athletes can and should have a positive impact on these outcomes.

Conclusion

Managing a college or university's cocurricular esports program is a complex task that will require a great deal of organization and effort, particularly on the part of the students involved and their adviser or coach. The primary keys to success will be preparation, organization, and flexibility. In addition, a program will need administrative support and buy-in from the campus to ultimately find success. Whether the program is housed in athletics, student affairs, or academic affairs, the students will need broad support. Unfortunately, as noted throughout this book, negative assumptions and stereotypes about esports athletes are real. A coach will need to serve as an advocate for the students and the sport to help ensure its success. Administrators—deans of students, athletic directors, and provosts in particular—will also need to help in this regard. Having the resources to properly provide for and manage the team is a huge first step, but the support and understanding will be what helps move a program from just existing on a campus to truly succeeding.

APPENDIX 3A
Schreiner University Gamer's Guild Creed

Article I: Identity

The name of this organization shall be the Schreiner University Gamer's Guild.

Article II: Purpose

The Gamer's Guild exists to enable like-minded individuals the opportunity to come together and experience the joys of computer, console, and hobby gaming. The enterprise will allow for growth in problem-solving, creative thinking, intellectual curiosity, and interpersonal relations. In addition, members will flourish emotionally, intellectually, and socially through these combined experiences. The Gamer's Guild will serve as a central community hub for all things gaming.

Article III: Membership

Section 1 Eligibility

One shall only be eligible for membership if they (1) are a bona fide student in full college standing in attendance at Schreiner University, (2) have achieved a 2.5 cumulative GPA throughout their college career.

Section 2 Election to New Membership

Membership to the Gamer's Guild is ad libitum.

Section 3 Status of Membership

All members of the Gamer's Guild shall be considered equal in standing and shall enjoy entirely the same rights, privileges, and responsibilities of membership.

Section 4 Revocation of Membership

The membership of a member may only be revoked through a formal and exact hearing in an official meeting of a judicial council or by the discretion of the Advisory Board.

Article IV: Organizational Structure

Section 1 Elected Officers

The elected officers of the Gamer's Guild shall be the President, Vice President of Computer Gaming, Vice President of Console Gaming, Vice President of Hobby Gaming, Secretary, Treasurer, and Public Relations Officer. The President, Vice President of Computer Gaming, Vice President of Console Gaming, Vice President of Hobby Gaming, Secretary, Treasurer, and Public Relations Officer shall make up the Gamer's Guild Executive Council.

Section 2 Advisory Board

The Advisory Board of the Gamer's Guild shall be the President of the Advisory Board, President of the Gamer's Guild, Adviser for Computer Gaming, Adviser for Console Gaming, Adviser for Hobby Gaming, and Varsity Sports Adviser. The Board shall oversee all affairs of the Gamer's Guild and be vested with supreme executive power over all internal and external decisions therein. The Board will report directly to the Chief Adviser of the Gamer's Guild.

Section 3 Terms of Office and Qualifications

The term of office of the elected officers shall be for no less than 355 days and no more than 375 days. (1) Each officer must have a cumulative collegiate GPA of no less than 2.75.

Section 4 Resignation

Officers may only resign with the approval of a simple majority vote of the Gamer's Guild or upon approval by the Advisory Board. Any vacancy occurring during the year shall be filled by a majority vote at the next official meeting of the Gamer's Guild. All duties and responsibilities of any resigning officer shall be the responsibility of the President until that position is duly filled.

Section 5 Removal From Office

The Gamer's Guild may remove a member from office through a seventy-five percent (75%) vote and approval of the Advisory Board. Such removal will take place immediately.

Section 6 Responsibilities

The duties of the elected officers shall include but are not limited to the following:

A. The **President** shall be the official head of the Gamer's Guild and shall have the following duties:

1. Preside at all meetings, preserving respect, order, and decorum;
2. Acquaint themselves thoroughly with the Charter and Laws of the Gamer's Guild, enforcing such rules rigidly;
3. Ensure that the Gamer's Guild utilizes the Advisory Board and continually promotes constant, positive, and appreciative weekly communication with the Board;
4. Promote positive communication with the institution's Student Activities Director, Dean, and other such administrator(s);
5. Oversee the productivity, responsibility, and accountability of all Gamer's Guild officers (i.e., success of committees through the Vice Presidents, accurate and timely reporting of the Secretary; positive fiscal status of the Gamer's Guild through the Treasurer;
6. Lead the membership through a comprehensive evaluation of the Gamer's Guild at the beginning of each academic term;
7. Lead the membership through a continuous goal development and tracking process.

B. The **Vice President of Computer Gaming (VP PC)** shall be one of three second officers thereof in rank, and shall oversee all committees pertaining to Computer Gaming.

1. Oversee all internal aspects of the Gamer's Guild Computer Gaming operations;
2. Ensure productivity and accountability of membership;
3. Appoint and oversee Computer Gaming committee chairs;

4. Ensure that Computer Gaming committee system functions and that actual committees operate smoothly;
5. Ensure participation and attendance at Gamer's Guild events;
6. Ensure that the membership is content with Gamer's Guild operations;
7. Ensure that the Gamer's Guild has (at the very minimum) the following actual committees: Computer Gaming Competitive Committee and Computer Gaming Recreation Committee.
8. Delegate duties to committee chairs and members.
9. Work with other Vice Presidents to facilitate bimonthly social events.

C. The **Vice President of Console Gaming (VP CG)** shall be one of three second officers thereof in rank, and shall oversee all committees pertaining to Console Gaming.

1. Oversee all internal aspects of the Gamer's Guild Console Gaming operations;
2. Ensure productivity and accountability of membership;
3. Appoint and oversee Console Gaming committee chairs;
4. Ensure that Console Gaming committee system functions and that actual committees operate smoothly;
5. Ensure participation and attendance at Gamer's Guild events;
6. Ensure that the membership is content with Gamer's Guild operations;
7. Ensure that the Gamer's Guild has (at the very minimum) the following actual committees: Console Gaming Competitive Committee and Console Gaming Recreation Committee.
8. Delegate duties to committee chairs and members.
9. Work with other Vice Presidents to facilitate bimonthly social events.

D. The **Vice President of Hobby Gaming (VP HG)** shall be one of three second officers thereof in rank and shall oversee all committees pertaining to Hobby Gaming.

1. Oversee all internal aspects of the Gamer's Guild Hobby Gaming operations;
2. Ensure productivity and accountability of membership;

3. Appoint and oversee Hobby Gaming committee chairs;
4. Ensure that Hobby Gaming committee system functions and that actual committees operate smoothly;
5. Ensure participation and attendance at Gamer's Guild events;
6. Ensure that the membership is content with Gamer's Guild operations;
7. Ensure that the Gamer's Guild has (at the very minimum) the following actual committees: Hobby Gaming Competitive Committee and Hobby Gaming Recreation Committee.
8. Delegate duties to committee chairs and members.
9. Work with other Vice Presidents to facilitate bimonthly social events.

E. The **Secretary** shall serve as an amanuensis to the Gamer's Guild. It is his duty to make official reports, take the minutes at Gamer's Guild meetings, ensure successful Association communication, and keep and preserve all records.

1. Complete all Gamer's Guild paperwork;
2. Record minutes from weekly Gamer's Guild meetings and distribute such minutes within 36 hours;
3. Maintain and distribute/conspicuously display a Guild calendar;
4. Create and distribute agendas for weekly Chapter meetings by soliciting announcements and topics of officer reports prior to the meeting;

F. The **Treasurer** shall be the comptroller of the association. They are responsible for the collection of all monies due the Gamer's Guild, and the payment of all bills incurred by the Gamer's Guild.

1. Oversee all areas of the Gamer's Guild finances and ensure the long-term fiscal health of the Gamer's Guild;
2. Oversee the creation of a Gamer's Guild budget for each academic term and for each fiscal year;
3. Ensure the tracking and timely collection of all accounts receivable, such as alumni contributions, fundraising checks, member fees and assessments, and fines;
4. Balance Gamer's Guild checkbooks and accounts each week;

5. Submit weekly budget-to-actual statements and balance sheets at every weekly Gamer's Guild meeting.

G. The **Public Relations Officer** shall manage all aspects of Gamer's Guild image. They are responsible for overseeing the positive promotion of the Gamer's Guild and all crests, insignia, and regalia therein.

1. Ensure a positive image of the Gamer's Guild is maintained and promoted throughout the University and surrounding community;
2. Utilize analog and digital means of communication to connect and network Gamer's Guild associates and pertinent University and community members;
3. Appoint and oversee committee chairs related to the management of Gamer's Guild image;
4. Ensure that the Gamer's Guild has (at the very minimum) the following actual committees: Service and Philanthropy Committee, Marketing Committee, and Fundraising Committee.
5. Delegate duties to committee chairs and members.

Article VII: Amendments

Section 1 Proposal of Amendments

Proposals for amendments to this constitution may originate in a motion sponsored by four (4) or more voting members.

Section 2 Procedure of Amendment

In order to take effect, any motion to amend must receive an affirmative vote of at least three-fifths of the voting membership at two official meetings of the Gamer's Guild separated by no less than six (6) days.

4

EXPERIENCES OF AN ESPORTS STUDENT-ATHLETE

We make the case throughout this book that successful esports programs in higher education keep the students at the forefront of consideration and decision-making. Doing so requires that higher education faculty and professionals have at least some familiarity with the experiences of the students who are involved in esports. What is it like to be an esports athlete while pursuing a college degree? How do they view their involvement in esports relative to their other roles on campus and in life? What are their interactions with family like when it comes to involvement in esports? In what ways, positively or negatively, does participating in esports impact their success in college? As we point out in chapter 6, one of the challenges for colleges and universities interested in offering successful curricular and cocurricular esports programming is a dearth of data. This includes the need for qualitative studies of the histories and experiences of student esports participants and fans.

This chapter presents the story of Ryan Arnett, an esports athlete throughout college and an avid player, streamcaster, and educator today, in his own words. After relating the experiences of this esports student-athlete, the chapter moves on to advice for colleges and universities from the perspective of a student-athlete about creating healthy and supportive esports programs that advance student success.

In the Beginning

I have been a gamer since before I can even remember. Games were always catching my interest as a child, but I didn't think they would lead me to where I am today. The earliest memories I have of playing video games are with my grandpa. I would wake up in the middle of the night and mistake the streetlights outside for daylight and wake him up to play Nintendo 64.

My grandpa was one of my biggest supporters when it came to my time playing video games. My mother, however, shared the concerns of many parents in the late 1990s when it came to their children and video games. She was worried about my health, rightfully. Video games and their more consistent players had a stigma of physical and mental problems surrounding them. Despite her worries, video games had very small negative impacts in my life until I got to high school.

I was at a college prep school and was struggling to balance my academics with fun. I was on academic probation after my first semester of high school, largely because of poor time management. I prioritized playing games and being with friends over completing schoolwork. I was placed in a structured study hall program at the school that put me in a proctored classroom with other students all doing work. We weren't allowed to be on our computers unless we had an assignment that required it, and some teachers would not even allow us to listen to music during the 2-hour period every night.

I can't say that this was fun, but it was effective. My GPA did a 180-degree turn over one semester, and I was no longer required to attend soon after the end of my second semester. Not everyone needs something this structured or extreme, but just being in a workplace instead of being in my room doing work boosted my productivity. It didn't stop me from gaming, but it helped me manage my game time with my other responsibilities.

Undergraduate Years

I was introduced to esports in my first year of college. My friends introduced me to League of Legends. After I got into the game, my friends also mentioned the esports league for the game. It wasn't long until I was as familiar with the teams and players in the League of Legends Championship Series (LCS) as I was with the teams and players in the National Hockey League. Although this was my first foray into the world of esports, this wasn't when I first got involved in the esports community as more than just a fan.

My first brush with taking part in organized esports came soon after graduating from undergrad. Overwatch was released the summer after my graduation, and I was quite good at the Xbox version. I began trying out for teams and getting my first taste of what it meant to be involved in the competitive aspect of esports. Nothing official came of this first exploration, mostly because I knew I would not be able to dedicate the time needed once I began law school. I did, however, learn a lot about esports structure, and I made a lot of friends in the process.

Law School Years

My first year of law school was tough and left me very little time to enjoy games the way that I used to. Toward the end of the first semester, however, I picked up on ways to complete tasks efficiently and leave myself more time to play some games with my friends. Gaming is a very effective way to spend time with friends with whom you can't spend time in person. I left a lot of friends when I left undergrad, and gaming was an easy way to keep in touch with them and do something with them. However, I found myself wanting to do more with esports than just hang out with friends.

That's when I bought my first gaming computer. I had always been a console player, but I wanted to try playing on a computer. I wasn't very good when I first started, but I knew most of the games I was playing from the console versions. That's when I truly got involved in esports; I became a caster and commented on and produced videos and live streams of Overwatch University League matches and that's when I got hooked. I was embedded into the competitive culture and it drove me to be involved with esports in other games as well.

It wasn't long after this that I started live streaming on my own channel after getting a taste from broadcasting for others. I waited until the summer after my first year of law school to begin streaming consistently, and that's when I met Chris ("Taksee") and Brian ("Bhink"). These two esports professional gamers took me under their wing and put me on the path to competitive gaming that I never thought possible. I was playing on my first esports team in about a year, thanks to their teaching and friendship.

Turning Pro and Being in Law School

When I was playing for Hog Pen, my esports team, there wasn't much on my mind besides the game and school. I was playing competitive PlayerUnknown's Battlegrounds while taking a full course load in law school. It was tough, but I really wanted both things. After a day of classes I would go home and immediately boot up my computer to do one of three things: play, watch, or read. After a couple hours of that, I would make dinner, eat, spend time with friends, and do any schoolwork I needed to do.

Then, I would spend the next 3 hours to 5 hours practicing with my teammates for 6 days out of the week. We weren't as good as or serious as the top tier pro teams, so missing practice was never a big deal, but we always showed up anyway. The drive and passion to get better and push to the next level had us showing up every night, even without a paid contract or large prize pools from tournaments.

Friendships and Life Lessons

These teammates became some of my good friends. We built bonds on the team that went beyond just being teammates. When I was in undergrad, I was part of a fraternity. The bond that I built with my teammates—whom I had never met in person—was strikingly similar to the bond I shared with my fraternity brothers. We didn't have any fancy rituals or mottos, but we had an understanding and a respect for one another. This respect was especially necessary for us as we disagreed on a lot of things about the game and all had different lifestyle choices.

We overcame any hardships and obstacles by focusing on our common objective of getting better as a team. That meant making individual sacrifices at times, such as putting in long hours, missing social gatherings, and staying in on weekend nights. All players on the team were at least 18 years old and lived on their own, so they had freedom to sacrifice. These weren't kids who had nothing better to do. We made our choices knowing those sacrifices, and I do not regret making those choices. I made lifelong bonds with my teammates. Those bonds may weaken over time, but they will not break. They will always be my teammates.

The friendship even extended beyond the boundaries of the internet for me and one of my teammates, Henrik ("Styleth"). Styleth is from Norway, and we decided to meet each other at a convention in Seattle, Washington, where we stayed in a hotel together for a few days and even took a day trip up to Vancouver. This goes to show that everlasting friendships can be built on esports teams even if the players aren't face-to-face. The friendships should be much easier to cultivate at higher education institutions because the students will all be in the same place. If I can make the friends that I did online, I can only imagine the bonds that teams will make when sharing the same playing and living space.

Sometimes, playing with others doesn't always lead to lifelong friendships, although it can lead to respect. I consistently butted heads with one of my teammates while playing for Hog Pen. We were friends and liked each other, but there were some situations (in-game) that we just viewed very differently. I was the captain of the team and took it upon myself to run practices. Practices included trying new strategies, putting ourselves in tough in-game situations, and doing things to hone specific skills that may not have made sense at the time to someone focused on winning every game. Some of my teammates would question what we were doing from time to time, and I always explained my thoughts and reasoning behind what we were doing. Sometimes those reasons were challenged, usually because the person did not think that what we were doing was useful. If we did the practice anyway, they would be upset; if I decided to change the practice, even if I didn't really want to, I would be upset.

We didn't let our feelings get in the way of our gameplay for the most part. At some points, during situations I had set up, our team would get frustrated. My teammates may have said things such as "Why are we even doing this?" But, in the end, we all knew that we wanted to get better as a team and climb in the competitive scene. As long as the team knows that everyone on the team is trying their best and putting in a good effort, it will garner respect. People don't have to like each other to respect each other. Two people with nothing in common except a skill in a particular video game can still make good teammates. Their chemistry may not be ideal, but the end goal and common focus can usually bring them together to compete with the same ability as two friends on a team.

The bond of a teammate is forged over more than just actual gameplay. We, as a team, spent hours reviewing our own gameplay and gameplay from other teams, similar to what a football or other traditional sports team does prior to a match. In PlayerUnknown's Battlegrounds, it was a little more difficult to scout teams because we would face so many different teams at once and teams would come and go from the league, but that became part of our regular routine. Esports is more than aiming accurately or reacting quickly. It is knowledge, critical thinking, and repetition as well.

Choices Made and Prices Paid

Unfortunately, after joining an esports team, my GPA did fall. I consciously made that decision though. I knew there would be readings that I didn't do, classes I wasn't prepared for, and assignments that I could have spent more time on. It wasn't an issue of putting my team and the game over school, but I did put them on a similar level. It was a tough decision every time I had to choose between finishing a chapter for class the next day or attending practice with the team.

The best way to keep yourself from falling into a downward spiral is to set boundaries for yourself (or for your students in the case of an institution). Boundaries I set for myself included things like only missing a reading for a class once a week, not practicing the night before a test or exam, and writing at least 250 words on a written assignment before practicing. Academic boundaries weren't the only type of boundaries I had to set, though.

I had no one to keep me in check or hold me accountable besides myself. That almost caused some issues going through law school, but I always managed to put myself back on my feet and moving in the right direction. Other people may need someone to hold them accountable and make sure that they do not fall too far. Without minimum academic requirements from NACE or their college, a student could be failing out of a semester and still be participating in an esports program.

Money Talks

Students receiving prize money may be affected more negatively than others. When there is a passion for something coupled with a monetary reward, it becomes easier for people to disregard other responsibilities. When I was playing PlayerUnknown's Battleground for Hog Pen, my contract was unpaid. There was no salary, no bonus for performing well in certain events, or anything like that. My only opportunity to get paid was to win prize money in a tournament. We, as the team, planned to split a percentage of the prize pool and donate the rest to the organization. We never won an event with a cash prize, so our plan never came to pass; however, we always wondered how the money would be spent by the organization if we were to win. Would they take it as a paycheck? Would they use the money to recruit members for another team? Would they try to hire an analyst or coach for us? Those questions never had to be asked, so they never got answered. We thought that the money would eventually be put back into the team, but it would have comforted us to know that we weren't just playing for the owners to have a payday.

Costs to Play Competitively

In part we wondered about prize money because playing games competitively can be expensive. Just like any other sport, there is equipment for esports players that is necessary or gives you an edge over other players. This equipment isn't necessarily cheap either. My setup included a $1,200 computer, a 144 Hz monitor, a gaming mouse and keyboard, and a pair of high-quality headphones. I also had a gaming chair that was meant to be sat in for long hours and blue light glasses to reduce eye strain and headaches while gaming. Gaming is just like any other sport. It can be done cheaply, but you get what you pay for. I sacrificed money for a competitive edge and physical comfort, and I would recommend that anyone make that sacrifice if they are able.

Taking Care of Yourself

I am guilty of letting things get cluttered pretty quickly, and it became overwhelming. I used to clean a little bit every day or so. Once I joined the team, I set myself a cleaning day with a 3-hour period so that I would keep my apartment from getting too messy. That gave me enough time to rein in the chaos if it had gone too far.

Other students may need additional personal health reminders. I have had friends who would go extraordinary hours behind the screen without taking breaks to move around, eat food, or drink water. Being an avid sports player, I kept myself physically in check. Some friends of mine would set timers on their phones or computers to remind them to take breaks and get nutrition. Schools may want to limit the amount of time a practice may go or enforce a break period.

Sleep is a critical component. I have gone a day or two without sleep here and there, but I have some friends who consistently only get 3 to 4 hours of sleep most nights. It's important to remember that sleep is one of the most critical aspects of our physical health and needs to be maintained. Improper self-care can lead to bad physical and mental health (see chapter 5 for more on this topic).

Esports Environment

Video games are surrounded by a stigma of toxic behavior, most often manifested as racist, misogynistic, or homophobic remarks through the in-game voice chat or text chat. It is a little less prevalent in the competitive scene for video games as the players are usually a little more professionally behaved due to possible repercussions from their organization or the league/tournament organizers. Although it's mostly prevalent in casual, online gaming, it is still present in competitive gaming as well. I have a friend who stopped competing in local LAN tournaments due to credible and aggressive death threats and sexually aggressive threats from the other team after a competition.

Socialization and Esports

Proper care also includes socialization, but that can also come from video games in proper dosages. Talking to people online or in person always came naturally to me; however, sometimes people, especially my parents, would question the friends that I made online. I was frequently told to "go make some real friends" by family and people in my life. I used to let it bother me until I realized that these people were (in some cases) my real friends. When you spend many hours a day for several days a week talking to someone, you end up getting to know that person better than some of the friends you have in person. Some of my best friends have risen out of an online meeting. Just because you are not face-to-face or in person does not mean that the social interactions you are having aren't real. A lot of gamers will spend more time talking to some friends online than they will talking to their friends or family in person.

Just because you can make these great friends and connections online doesn't mean you should shun personal social interactions, though. It gets lonely without spending time with people in person. There were times when my only social time was with people online or in the classroom, and it isn't a substitute for spending time out with your friends.

Stereotypes and Esports

It's not just the friendships that are questioned though. I can't help but chuckle when people tell me things like "Oh, you don't look like a gamer" or "Do you ever talk to real people?" People have this idea that gamers are recluses who don't do anything or know anything outside of gaming. Even some gamers think this way too. The amount of times people are surprised that I play sports and still go to the gym are countless. It's like people formed an image of a gamer in the mid-1990s, and some refuse to let that image fade.

There are some people who fit the image I described, though, and it's not healthy. Prolonged screen time with no other human interaction or physical exercise is not good, and it's not something to be proud of. Some of my gaming friends boast about the hours they go without sleep, relying on coffee and energy drinks. I tell them to get some sleep every time, but for every person whose choices lend credence to the stereotype, there are countless others who live very normal and healthy lives.

Esports After College

Esports and gaming continue to be a big part of my life after law school. I still play games and live stream them. I strive to be the best I can competitively, and I am constantly looking for opportunities to broadcast league matches and tournaments. Additionally, I discovered that I can focus my career in esports. While I was getting my Juris Doctor from Stetson University College of Law, I took a sports law class that opened my eyes to sports and entertainment law. I immediately saw the opportunities in esports and decided to pursue the legal issues surrounding the esports and gaming industry. I became an agent for a few friends and their streaming channels. I contact companies for purposes of negotiation, advise clients on the best ways to network for endorsements and sponsorships, and am involved in many other facets. I have recently stepped back a bit from the agent role to focus more on the law and academia.

Recommendations for Colleges and Universities

Although I was not competing as an esports player for a school while in college, I was competing while a student. I have a lot of experience with management and balance between esports and school, and in this section I share my thoughts of what a good experience would look like for a student-athlete competing as a member of a college or university esports team.

The main things that institutions are going to want to focus on when it comes to their students are their physical and mental well-being, the handling of prize money, and socialization. If an institution can manage these aspects well, it may not guarantee the success of the program, but it will help the students have a smooth experience within the esports program or club. Students are not as worried about increasing enrollment, driving profits for the school, or school prestige as the staff implementing and running the program, but students are fundamental to achieving these goals.

Mental and Physical Health

Injuries and other physical ailments occur in esports. Players can suffer from wrist and hand injuries such as carpal tunnel syndrome, back pains from prolonged sitting without proper lumbar support, eye strain that can lead to migraines or other head and eye problems from prolonged screen time without protection, and a number of other things.

The easiest way to keep the physical health of an esports player up is to limit screen time, time seated without activity, and gameplay. Colleges and universities can put these moderation tactics into effect through a team coach or captain who can enforce the moderation. Some examples include a 10- to 15-minute break in the middle of a team practice to make sure that the students are not seated for too long without activity. This becomes especially important when it is factored in that most students are sitting without activity throughout their classes during the day as well. This example would also give the players' eyes a break from the blue light emitted from the screens.

Another way to maintain the physical well-being of students is to provide proper equipment. Glasses that protect eyes from blue light, gaming chairs that are specifically designed for back and arm support, mice that fit players' hands comfortably, and proper desk height are all things that can be provided to a player to lower their chances of suffering physical ailments.

One of the toughest challenges that schools will likely face when attempting to care for players' physical health is that the players may not want things changed. Most players who are ready to play competitively have developed a routine that allows them to get better the best way they know how even if it means that the player plays 10 hours a day, never goes to the gym, and has a diet that consists of fast food and soda. Those are going to likely be the players who push back the hardest against physical health implementations, but also the players who will benefit from it the most.

Another option is to have a physical aspect of practice. It is simple to add in a day of aerobic or even nonaerobic exercises to keep a team or group fresh and in good physical condition. The benefits of good physical condition in relation to esports include things such as remaining calm with an elevated heart rate, increased resistance to physical ailments, and more precise muscle control. Physical exercise can also be beneficial for a player's mental health.

Mental health of a player should also be a concern of the school. Competitive video games are often decided by small margins and mistakes. Although seemingly small to an outside viewer, these mistakes can weigh heavily on an esports player's mind the same way missing an open net from 5 feet away in soccer would affect a soccer player's mind. On top of that, there are also concerns of accountability, priorities, and responsibilities.

Moderation of gameplay times, while being a physical bonus, can also be a mental bonus. If players are playing a game for 4 to 8 hours a day for 7 days a week, they are going to get burnt out and frustrated. They don't have time to mentally reset and come back to practice fresh. They also do not have the time to properly reflect on and release the frustrations and tensions that come about through competitive gaming.

Some ways to implement this sort of strategy would be gameplay breaks during practices. These breaks don't have to be free time either. The breaks can be studying game film, strategizing for an upcoming match, or a number of other things. These examples allow the players to have a break from intensive, competitive gameplay but still benefit the team by practicing in another way.

A player in poor mental health can be a detriment to the team as well as themselves. If a player is constantly in a bad mood, there is an increased possibility of lashing out at teammates, poor performance, lack of dedication, and other consequences. That is why it is important for a school and its esports program to implement mental health–focused programs before it becomes a problem.

While I was competing, I didn't have a coach or a school to tell me when or how to do things. I trusted in myself, my teammates, and those around me to guide me and hold me accountable when I needed it. If I were playing for a school team, I would expect the same mental and physical care and respect that is afforded to the other students playing traditional sports. I would expect to be provided equipment that wouldn't cause me physical discomfort at all times, and I would expect my coach not to force me to play a game for 8 hours a day. In the end, not all students will respond to programs the same way, but it is still going to fall on the schools to do their best to care for their students.

Prize Money

Prize money is inherently not allowed to go to the students in most other sports due to rules related to amateurism (see chapter 6 for a more extended discussion). Esports differs from those sports in the sense that students may well have already earned money from the sport, and NACE, the largest higher education esports association, does not prohibit student esports athletes from earning money from either college team prizes or competition outside of their college team. Other tournament and league organizers may restrict the amount of money going to students or the form in which that money is paid out (e.g., scholarships versus straight cash payouts), so it is important that an institution is aware of what the rules are for each different league and tournament. Having the ability to win prize money can affect the dedication of the students or cause a rift between esports players or between esports players and other student-athletes, besides creating trust issues with the school. This could be a particular problem for institutions that include the esports program under their athletic department and want all of the teams to be one cohesive unit.

Dedication can be swayed by the ability to earn prize money. One thing that drives players, including myself, to perform to the best of their ability is a possible payday. Schools are largely in charge of the prize money that is available to esports players from participating in collegiate tournaments. If a school doesn't give a student any money, it could lead to a lower drive to compete to the best of the student's ability. If a school gives some of the money, student dedication may increase. If the school gives most or all of the money, player dedication could increase even more, but it could cause other problems.

When the students aren't receiving the prize money they earn, there are likely going to be questions about where that money went and how it was spent. Students don't necessarily have the right to know where all of the money went specifically, but a lack of transparency could create distrust between the students and the staff. A student team that doesn't trust the staff or the school that it's representing is unlikely to perform at the best of its ability.

Whatever a school chooses to do with prize money earned that is able to be given to students, that school would most likely benefit from transparency to some degree. A student will not likely be looking for an itemized list of every dollar that was taken from the prize money, but they will want to know if the money is being used to get better equipment, or anything else for that matter. Students will also be less likely to take an institution at its word if it says it is putting money back into the program without any visible results. Therefore, it may be in a school's best interest to pick an easily visible upgrade or reward for the program that can be attained after a few tournament wins to earn the full respect of the students in the program. Even if the students aren't receiving a monetary payout, their dedication is likely to remain intact as long as they know they are benefiting somehow.

Socialization

Socialization issues are one of the main criticisms of the gaming and esports industry. People see gamers as introverted and unsociable creatures. Fortunately, this image isn't fully accurate. Socialization is very real and in depth when playing games online, and teammates will also likely socialize with each other. However, players should have a certain amount of live interaction in person and make sure that none of their social interactions are subject to toxic behavior.

Online socialization is more widely accepted than it used to be, but it is still not seen as true socialization by some people. The internet has grown in tremendous ways that have allowed people to become close friends with each other without ever coming face-to-face. This obviously causes issues from time to time (e.g., false identities), but it is not uncommon for people to have made good friends, or even a best friend, through online interaction. Gaming is part of that growth too. The multiplayer nature of online games and the ability to chat and connect with other players through the game or other programs make socialization over the internet a very real possibility. Serious gamers who spend a lot of time on the internet probably spend more time talking with others than do many non-gamers.. Socialization is no longer a thing consisting only of face-to-face interactions with the people around you. On the other hand, if someone is only socializing from behind a screen and rarely or never getting in-person socialization, it can be a problem.

Internet socialization cannot fully replace in-person socialization, even if it is a good substitute at times. Internet socialization only really uses the two senses of sight and hearing. The human body thrives off the sensual stimuli from social interactions that use touch, smell, and taste. Furthermore, someone who only socializes behind a screen loses or at least fails to strengthen the ability to read the facial and other nonverbal cues that are important in everyday conversation.

Another consideration of online socialization is that people are more likely to say things on the internet that they wouldn't say in person. When sitting behind a screen, there are no immediate facial reactions to show a person what they said was not a good thing to say. Furthermore, because they are not in the physical vicinity of the other person, they have the option to ignore the situation altogether. In a physical interaction, people have to see these reactions and deal with them in real time; they don't have 10 minutes to think about a message to send before they send it. Therefore, although internet socialization is real socialization, it is not a complete replacement for human interaction.

In an esports program on campus, teammates will likely socialize with each other on their own; even so, it may be a good idea to start a new season with icebreakers or have team-building exercises throughout the semester or year. It is also beneficial for people to meet new people, so the program would benefit from encouraged socialization with other groups inside or outside of the esports program.

The one thing to watch out for in all forms of socialization is toxic behavior. Most leagues and tournaments have restrictions on that sort of behavior from competitors, but general gameplay is full of toxicity. The most common forms of toxic behavior come in the form of harmful threats; general bullying; and racial, misogynistic, or homophobic slurs.

It is a good idea for schools to implement a toxic behavior rule for their esports programs or clubs on campus. If a student posts online using slurs or bullying another player and they are associated with an institution, the fault and consequences are going to lie, at least partially, with that institution. Although it is important to keep all types of toxic behavior eradicated, the most important are credible threats of harm. These harmful threats can include death threats, threats to fight after a LAN event, swatting, and anything else that could put another person in a harmful situation in the immediate future.

Team-to-team toxicity is prevalent in the gaming industry. Communication within a team, especially if two teammates don't particularly get along, should be monitored as well. Berating for underperforming is the most common form of toxic behavior among teammates. The most unfortunate side effects of this are that the player may feel that they no longer belong on the team and their performance can suffer. There is a difference between constructive criticism and bullying. It will be up to the colleges and universities to make sure that it doesn't cross the line.

This sort of behavior isn't the only toxicity that schools should worry about within a program. Hazing is common in fraternities, sororities, sports teams, and other close-knit groups. Esports programs are not exempt from the possibilities of hazing. A group of people spending many hours a day together during practice and competition are likely to also be together outside of those hours. When a bond like that forms, it is prone to "entry fees" in the form of hazing for newcomers. Hazing has led to deaths in the past and contributed to people leaving or being barred from a group (Data Team, 2017). It is necessary to make sure all students feel like they can be a part of the team without having to go through an arbitrary ritual that could cause them harm or discomfort.

Conclusion

It falls on the institutions to figure out what works best for their program as there is not a tried-and-true model for collegiate esports or esports clubs on campus yet. A school can have an esports program, but without students who are passionate and able to succeed, it will fail. As Steve Kerr, former chief learning officer for General Electric and Goldman Sachs, pointed out, "If you want something to happen, you have to make people able and you have to make them want to" (quoted in Partners in Leadership, n.d., para. 12). There are many things to think about when it comes to the well-being of the students in an esports program. Not every student is going to have the same issues and opportunities, but the ones detailed here will likely be among the most common.

5

ETHICAL, LEGAL, AND GOVERNANCE CONSIDERATIONS FOR ESPORTS PROGRAMS ON CAMPUS

Colleges and universities have unique roles and responsibilities in society. Ethical, legal, and governance considerations are attendant to those roles and responsibilities and, in a healthy and robust institution, ought to be exercised and demonstrated consistently across all domains of policy, practice, and programs. As an emerging area of higher education programming, attention should be given to matters of ethics, law, and governance as they relate to esports. This chapter will identify and discuss a number of these matters.

Homophobia, Misogyny, and Racism in Esports

A 2017 Pew Research study reported 41% of adults in the United States have been subjected to online harassment, and 61% of adults have witnessed others being harassed online (Adinoff & Türkay, 2018). Online gaming environments are specifically identified in the report as one of the cyberspaces in which this conduct is taking place. Adinoff and Türkay (2018) cited a number of studies indicating the deleterious effects of online harassment. Normalization of harassing behavior, victims becoming perpetrators, and aversion to involvement in online gaming are among the effects identified.

Some have described online gaming, particularly esports, as having a toxic climate for people who identify as members of the LGBTQ community, women, and members of minoritized racial or ethnic communities (Adinoff & Türkay, 2018; Consalvo, 2012). Donaldson (2017) termed the behavior creating this toxic or hostile climate as *deviant play*, which he described as being outside the designs of the game and social norms. Donaldson noted that deviant play (or speech, as we assert in the case of in-person or online spectators) is socially constructed and is the subject of continuous ongoing social negotiation.

We recognize that *toxicity*, *deviant play*, or whatever term you want to use can include broader problems related to a lack of civility on the part of players or spectators. However, we believe it is important to name and directly address three issues we see as being at the core of a lot of this conduct: homophobia, misogyny, and racism. We are not alone in this view. Funk et al. (2018) observed, "At their best, eSports can be exciting, competitive tournaments enjoyed in social settings. Unfortunately, eSports can also be plagued by racism, misogyny, and homophobia" (p. 12).

There are ethical and legal responsibilities related to a college or institution incorporating activities into their curricular and cocurricular programming. Institutions need to carefully consider those responsibilities relative to matters of harassment and equal opportunity when it comes to esports. This is not to say that colleges and universities should not involve themselves in esports programming; it does mean that those doing so must be cognizant of the environment to which their student-athletes and employees may be exposed and to work appropriately, inclusively, and proactively to address the challenges.

Homophobia

Dominique McLean is exceptional. One of the best esports players in the fighting game genre (including the arcade fighting game FighterZ), McLean was named the 2018 Game Awards' Esports Player of the Year (Van Allen, 2019). Their substantial accomplishments as an esports professional athlete are also notable in that McLean identifies as Black, nonbinary, furry, and male.

> The world of fighting games has always been more inclusive than the larger esports landscape in certain ways: racial diversity is a hallmark of the scene, due in large part to its roots in urban arcades. Yet, casual misogyny and homophobia linger still, energies that help make McLean a target of resentment as much as an emblem of progress. (Van Allen, 2019, para. 34)

Sadly, McLean's experiences being subjected to harassment based on their sexual orientation are not unique in esports. Austin Wilmont, an openly gay professional player, was the target of a homophobic comment in 2018 from another player (Gunn, 2019). That player was fined and suspended by the Overwatch League for his conduct toward Wilmont (Zavaleta, 2018). The incident is similar to one in which a Counter-Strike: Global Offensive player was suspended from Twitch for a month for directing a homophobic slur at another person online (Myers, 2018).

James ("Stress") O'Leary, a former European League of Legends caster who is out and who has been subjected to antigay diatribes in online esports settings, said that in his experience much of the hate speech toward marginalized people comes in chat rooms, forums, and the like (Bell, 2019). O'Leary stated, "Online communities inherently are dehumanized. You can't see somebody's face. You can't look into their eyes. You can't connect with them on an emotional level. That's why some people find it easy to throw out negative comments" (quoted in Bell, 2019, para. 21). We also find ourselves wondering whether the challenges in homophobia are, at least in part, a function of unhealthy constructions of masculinity and the developing gender identities of many of those involved in playing esports.

It is not surprising that in the face of harassment and marginalization LGBTQ members of the esports community (players and fans) have connected with one another for affirmation and support, adopting the term *gaymer* for themselves. It appears that at least esports business interests recognize the challenge that homophobia presents to the future of their industry and are taking steps to build a more inclusive culture in esports. A number of esports game titles, including Overwatch, Mortal Kombat, Dragon Age, and Grand Theft Auto, include LGBTQ characters (Gunn, 2019). The Overwatch League held its second Pride Day (Bell, 2019) in 2019, and Gay Games XI will include esports when it is held in 2022 in Hong Kong (Brigham, 2019).

Misogyny

Jackson (2016) noted that women have been involved in esports from almost the earliest days and they continue to be an active presence today as both players and fans. Soleil ("Ewok") Wheeler is 13 years old, deaf, and a young woman playing professional esports (Liao, 2019). Wheeler, who has 200,000 followers on Twitch and is known for play in Fortnite, recently became the first female member of Faze Clan, one of the most famous and selective esports organizations in the world. Like Dominique McLean's, hers is a remarkable story of accomplishment, and yet she has been the subject of online harassment as a woman playing in a sport that is dominated by men. Despite there being a number of women who play Fortnite, none were among the 178 finalists at the 2019 World Cup in New York. Wheeler, who recently played Fortnite alongside international esports star Tyler ("Ninja") Blevins, said,

> Gender doesn't matter in this. The important thing is to support each other while you're playing. So it felt really cool, it was a really unique experience. But I wanted to show Ninja that anyone can play. Male, female, it doesn't matter. (quoted in Liu, 2019, para. 10)

The gaming culture toward women has also been described as toxic (Consalvo, 2012). Gamergate, an example of toxic behavior that took place over a protracted period of time, is often mentioned when discussing this problem. Gamergate happened in 2014 when a group of people online began using the hashtag #Gamergate to harass several women in the online gaming industry, including game developers and journalists who had addressed issues of sexism in gaming (Dewey, 2014). The harassment included accusations of unprofessional conduct and inappropriate personal conduct, offensive language used in the course of taking issue with feminist perspectives, and threats of violence and sexual assault.

Banet-Weiser and Miltner (2016) pointed out the intersectional nature of the harassment.

> We are in a new era of gender wars, an era that is marked by alarming amounts of vitriol directed toward women in online spaces. These forms of violence are not only about gender, but are also often racist, with women of color as particular targets. (p. 171)

They termed this behavior *networked misogyny*. They went on to add:

> Arthur Chu, The Daily Beast's columnist on all things geek and nerd, has blamed this state of affairs on a culture that teaches geeky young men that "women, like money and status, are just part of the reward we get for doing well," and that popular misogyny is part of the (unwarranted) response when these men "get good grades, they get a decent job, and that wife they were promised in the package deal doesn't arrive" (Arthur Chu, 2014). However, what Chu and others have failed to note is that #GamerGate and other incidents of weaponized misogyny are not simply a response to entitlements that never came to fruition. They are also a response to the incursion of women and people of color into what were previously almost exclusively white, male spaces. (p. 172)

Ruvalcaba et al. (2018), making a similar point, argued, "eSports are not exempt from existing societal gender issues related to sexism and exclusion" (p. 296). They noted, however, "Despite the low number of female eSport pro players and the perception that women are not hard-core gamers, evidence suggests that female gamers perform equally well in online games when equal time is spent practicing" (p. 297). Ruvalcaba et al. highlighted a number of studies indicating a relationship between playing video games, particularly ones with gender-stereotyped images, and accepting sexual harassment. They identified anonymity of online spaces as facilitating harassment and discrimination, citing a study in which nearly half of the adolescents who play video games reported experiences with hateful, racist, sexist behavior in online gaming. Continuing their review of research related to the experiences of women in esports, Ruvalcaba et al. reported studies showing women get more body-related messages in streaming and men get more game-related messages, the negative impact of sexual harassment on female athlete performances, and the impact of messages to women players saying women are not as good at esports as men. In their own study, Ruvalcaba et al. reported mixed evidence regarding comments during online gaming. Men perceived themselves as getting more positive feedback during online gaming from other men, and women saw the same in terms of getting more positive feedback from women. However, when Ruvalcaba et al. actually observed comments made during online gaming sessions, there were no differences in the amount of negative comments directed toward men and women. More positive comments were directed toward women, and women were far more likely to be the target of sexual comments than men.

Title IX

Higher education institutions engaged in esports programming, whether curricular or cocurricular, should be sensitive to matters of equal opportunity and inclusivity for all students. They must take special care, however, to be sure that the programs and services of the institution are in compliance with Title IX of the Educational Amendment Act of 1972. Title IX prohibits discrimination on the basis of sex in any education activity receiving federal financial support (including any program at a college or university that accepts federal financial aid dollars, federal research funding, or federal funding for student success programs like Trio). Space constraints do not allow for a full discussion of Title IX here, but it is important to recognize that many of the complaints filed alleging violations of Title IX relate to matters of intercollegiate athletics or issues of harassment (Kaplin et al., 2019).

Title IX addresses all programs and services of a higher education institution, both curricular and cocurricular. In regard to athletics, "the regulation requires institutions to operate unitary teams [teams open to members of both sexes] only for non-contact sports for which selection is non-competitive" (Kaplin et al., 2019, p. 1478). Club teams (assuming they hold competitive tryouts) and intercollegiate varsity athletics lie outside that requirement.

No matter whether they offer unitary or separate teams, colleges and universities must ensure equal opportunity for both sexes across all their athletic offerings. The finding in *Cohen v. Brown* (1993) provided a three-part test that serves to this day in determining whether equal opportunity exists, with an institution needing to meet at least one of the three parts:

1. Whether intercollegiate level participation opportunities for male and female students are provided in numbers substantially proportionate to their respective enrollments; or
2. Where the members of one sex have been and are underrepresented among intercollegiate athletes, whether the institution can show a history and continuing practice of program expansion which is demonstrably responsive to developing interest and abilities of the members of that sex; or
3. Where the members of one sex have been and are underrepresented among intercollegiate athletes, and the institution cannot show a continuing practice of program expansion such as cited above, whether it can be demonstrated that the interests and abilities of the members of that sex have been fully and effectively accommodated by the present program [44 Fed. Reg. at 71418]. (quoted in Kaplin et al., 2019, p. 1481)

It will be interesting to see how courts handle esports when it comes to assessing whether or not higher education institutions are meeting the three-part test. It appears that most esports programs in higher education today, both club teams and varsity, are operating on a unitary basis. What happens when colleges and universities open their teams to both sexes, but men pursue the opportunities in far greater numbers and hold most of the spots on a team? What happens if schools decide to have two teams, but their women's team competes in far fewer games because of interest? Here we may see higher education and the courts turn to 34 C.F.R. §106.41(c), which enumerates 10 factors for measuring the equality of athletic offerings:

1. Whether the selection of sports and levels of competition effectively accommodate the interests and abilities of members of both sexes
2. The provision of equipment and supplies
3. Scheduling of games and practice time
4. Travel and per diem allowance
5. Opportunity to receive coaching and academic tutoring
6. Assignment and compensation of coaches and tutors
7. Provision of locker rooms and practice and competitive facilities
8. Provision of medical and training facilities and services
9. Provision of the housing and dining facilities and services
10. Publicity (quoted in Kaplin et al., 2019, p. 1478)

Title IX's consideration of climate and discrimination turns on two points—quid pro quo harassment and chilly climate. Quid pro quo harassment may involve granting or withholding opportunities or the imposing negative consequences when one party either acquiesces to or rebuffs another party's otherwise unwanted and unwelcome social advances. Chilly climate harassment occurs when behavior based on sex is such that a person feels uncomfortable in an educational setting and unable to take equal advantage of the learning opportunity otherwise available. A chilly climate may be created either through one or two significantly offensive behaviors or through an ongoing series of less significant (but still impactful) behaviors. In regard to harassment, the case *Davis v. Monroe County Board of Education* (1999) is of particular importance. The court articulated a four-part test through which institutional liability for student-on-student harassment can be evaluated:

1. The institution must have "actual knowledge" of the harassment;
2. The institution must have responded (or failed to respond) to the harassment with "deliberate indifference," which the Davis Court defines as a response that is "clearly unreasonable in light of the known circumstances" (526 U.S. at 648);
3. The institution must have had "substantial control" over the student harasser and the context of the harassment; and
4. The harassment must have been "severe, pervasive, and objectively offensive" to an extent that the victim of the harassment was in effect deprived of educational opportunities or services. (quoted in Kaplin et al., 2019, pp. 1890–1891)

It is, unfortunately, all too easy to imagine a harassment situation. Picture a college esports team competing online in the school's esports arena. The contest is being streamed on the institutional computing infrastructure, and one or more of the student spectators begins directing online comments toward the lone woman who is a member of the opposing team—or even of the home team. Consider that scenario in light of the *Davis* test.

Racism

Terrence ("TerrenceM") Miller, an African American professional esports player, was competing in the Hearthstone tournament at DreamHack Austin in 2016. It was particularly special because his parents were watching the event on the Twitch stream (Mulkerin, 2016). When the racist comments about their son became overwhelming, they set the screen to full video so as to no longer have to read what was being spewed as part of the broadcast.

The problem of racism in esports is not directed solely toward African Americans. As has been noted earlier in this chapter, members of other racially or ethnically minoritized groups are subjected to similar odious online conduct. Peterson (2018) addressed the underrepresentation of African Americans in the ranks of esports professional athletes. Noting data from ESPN showing fans by ethnicity (see Figure 5.1), Peterson observed that African Americans are less present in the pro player pools than one would otherwise expect.

According to Peterson (2018), one reason may be the two primary platforms on which esports are played—PCs and consoles. Peterson, referencing research by Georgia Tech researcher Betsy DiSalvo, noted that African American males tend to play on consoles. Prize pools and sponsorships are larger for PC-based games. Consoles play a bit differently, and Peterson suggested that there may be differences in socioeconomic status between players who are able to access esports via PC and those who have the opportunity to play using a console, and she pointed to some areas of esports where intentional efforts are made to ensure opportunities for both PC and console players.

Higher Education's Obligation and Opportunity

"Whether it stems from a disconnect caused by technology, unrecognized privilege, or the current political climate" (Alonzo, 2019, para. 8), hostility and harassment in esports are additional obstacles for LGBTQ people, women, and people of color that straight, male, cisgendered, White players are not forced to confront (Mulkerin, 2016).

Most of the examples used in this section of the chapter are drawn from the world of professional esports. There is very little in either academic or popular literature related to the challenges of homophobia, misogyny, and racism

Figure 5.1. Esports fans by ethnicity.

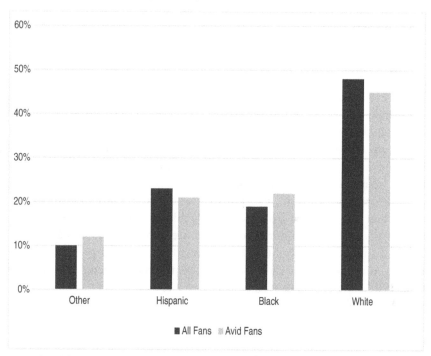

Note. Adapted from Peterson (2018).

specifically in esports in higher education, but we believe that it is reasonable to assume that those behaviors also exist in that context. We hypothesize that the challenges of the culture of online gaming and esports begin in the early experiences of young players as they explore the games online, and we further suggest that the troubling behaviors are reinforced throughout the learning life of the player unless deliberately and purposefully redirected through thoughtful education and leadership. Alonzo (2019) quoted an African American pro player and team leader as saying,

> I think ignoring toxic behaviour is something that people do much too often, especially in gaming communities, where it's been seen as something that's more normalized. But if the person doing said behaviour isn't being called out for it, who's to say that they even know that what they're doing is wrong? (para. 16)

We believe higher education institutions that include esports among their curricular and cocurricular offerings have an obligation and opportunity to address these issues in esports and, through those efforts, in society as a whole, not through calling people out but through calling them in. The obligation stems from our unique roles and responsibilities addressed at the onset of this chapter. The opportunity is reflected in the research on how college affects students. Mayhew et al. (2016) described the evidence of higher education's ability to impact students' attitudes and diversity as mixed but generally positive. Research shows mixed results regarding diversity development during college, with modest gains on measures of universality/diversity and pluralistic orientation but modest losses on commitment to racial understanding. There is evidence of positive growth with regard to progressive gender-role ideologies and attitudes toward lesbian, gay, and bisexual people. Structural diversity, peer culture, and curricular diversity engagement are all features of the college experience associated with positive gains, where they exist.

Jackson (2016) has presented several suggestions for ways in which colleges and universities can create esports programs that are inclusive and respectful. One notable recommendation is to make teams unitary (coed) with respect to gender and ensuring that this is not a "for show" status with just one or two women players. Two others are adopting an esports code of conduct and centering student leadership throughout esports programs.

Another step that could be taken is to give thoughtful consideration to the games in which esports teams compete. Some games are more inclusive than others. Overwatch, for example, has a diverse group of 28 heroes (Alonzo, 2019). Other games make use of positive reinforcement for players who engage inclusively by offering points or other in-game rewards, and yet others make use of priming messages that encourage positive and inclusive play as the games load (Adinoff & Türkay, 2018).

The University of California at Irvine (UCI) takes a thoughtful and thorough approach to matters of inclusion in their esports program. The UCI Code of Conduct uses clear and concise language in saying what is valued and what is prohibited, and it calls on everyone to take ownership through reporting behavior that may violate the code. The language is consistently and prominently presented to players, staff, fans, and others (UCI Esports, n.d.). It reads as follows:

We welcome and respect gamers of all types, from all places and backgrounds.

1. Harassment based on any aspect of a person's identity will not be tolerated.
2. No "toxicity" allowed. Behaviors that create an intolerable environment such as bullying threats of violence, stalking, or other forms of intimidation will not be tolerated.
3. No cheating or illegal activity allowed.
4. If you see something, say something. (para. 2)

The code of conduct is linked to extant institutional and systems policies and principles for community and inclusion, anchoring it in the context of broader institutional principles and values.

UCI also has an inclusivity plan (UCI Esports, 2017), the product of an Inclusion in Esports Task Force established in 2017. The task force included representatives from students, senior administration, alumni, faculty, and staff. The plan describes accomplishments and intentions in the areas of student-athlete recruitment as well as staff, curriculum, academic and cocurricular programming, and community outreach.

Colleges and universities might also consider working with esports game publishers and online broadcasting companies to report unacceptable behavior. These industry entities have an interest in helping ensure that their products are welcoming and inclusive, and they have a variety of tools at their disposal that are not available to higher education institutions.

> The most common form of punishment in esports games is the ban. This blocks the offender's account from logging into the game. Bans may last a day or two, weeks, or in the case of repeat or egregious offences, permanently. Another form of punishment is restricting the use of in game voice or text. (Adinoff & Türkay, 2018, p. 367)

Free Speech

The question of using negative reinforcements as a strategy for addressing hateful or hurtful behavior (including expressive behavior) in esports is just one example of esports-related activities requiring consideration of First Amendment issues in esports curricular or cocurricular programs. This section explores several of these activities. Although addressing matters of law and policy, nothing in this section should be construed as legal advice. Higher education professionals finding themselves dealing with legal matters are advised to consult with counsel for their college or university.

Sun and McClellan (2019) stated,

> There is little doubt based on long-standing legal precedent that the First Amendment right of free speech is present in the curricular and cocurricular life of students at public institutions of higher education as a matter of Constitutional law, and freedoms fashioned after those provided for in the First Amendment are commonly extended to students at privately-controlled colleges and universities as a matter of institutional policy and through various contracts between the student and the institution. (pp. 64–65)

Taking note of the legal distinction between public and private institutions addressed in the remarks by Sun and McClellan, the terms *First Amendment* and *free speech* will be used throughout this section to refer to both the constitutional freedoms guaranteed at public institutions and those freedoms fashioned after the Constitution that are commonly extended by contract as well as local and state laws at private institutions.

The presence of free speech rights in higher education is beyond question, but the interpretation and application of those rights are often matters of dispute and litigation. These disagreements commonly center around one or more of the following circumstances:

- Does the speech fit into one or more of the categories of speech outside of the First Amendment?
- Is the speech under the purview of the institutions (i.e., is it internal or external)?
- Did the speech occur in a space designated for certain types of expressive activities?
- How, if at all, does the nature of digital speech (computer-mediated and taking place using a LAN or the internet) impact whether or not the expressive behavior is protected?

Exempted Speech

There are several forms of speech that are not protected as free speech, including fighting words, threats and intimidation, obscenity, defamation, and harassment (PEN America, 2017). Each of these will be briefly described.

The legal doctrine of fighting words is commonly traced to *Chaplinsky v. New Hampshire* (1942). The doctrine has evolved through a series of subsequent cases to its current construction as speech directed at a person that is likely to provoke an immediate physical action. Despite being commonly referenced, it should be noted there are no recent higher education legal cases in which the court has ruled the speech in question to be fighting words.

Two important cases can help in understanding the ways in which courts view threatening and intimidating speech. First, the decision in *Virginia v. Black* (2003) described a true threat as

> reflecting the intent of the person speaking to express a serious intent to commit violence against an individual or group of individuals, including such expressions for the purpose of intimidation. That definition follows in the tradition of decisions that focus on whether or not the expression in question is clear, direct, and serious in intent. (quoted in Sun & McClellan, 2019, p. 66)

The second case, *Planned Parenthood of Columbia/Willamette, Inc., et al. v. American Coalition of Life Advocates, et al.* (2002), is important in that the court held that encouraging violence is protected speech, but threatening someone with violence is not.

In regard to defining *obscenity*, Supreme Court Justice Potter Stewart famously opined in *Jacobellis v. Ohio* (1964) that he would know it when he saw it. *Miller v. California* (1973) offers more practical, though sometimes vexing, criteria for determining obscene speech. The court determined that

> obscenity must depict or describe sexual conduct as specifically defined in applicable law and must, when taken on the whole, appeal to prurient sexual interest, portray sexual conduct in a patently offensive way, and (again, when taken on the whole) have no serious literary, artistic, political, or scientific value. (quoted in Sun & McClellan, 2019, p. 67)

The definition of *defamation* is succinct in the eyes of the courts.

> Common law and constitutional doctrines require that (1) the statement be false; (2) the publication serve to identify the particular person libeled; (3) the publication cause at least nominal injury to the person libeled; usually including but not limited to injury to reputation; and (4) the falsehood be attributed to some fault on the part of the person or organization publishing it. (quoted in Kaplin & Lee, 2013, p. 1320)

Specifically in regard to esports and the streaming of esports, colleges and universities may want to consider the ways in which courts have handled institutional liability for student publications. "Greater liability comes when a college or university sponsors the publication, the editorial staff is employed by the institution, and when the institution exercises some form of formal advanced review of content prior to publication" (Sun & McClellan, 2019, p. 67). So, if the institution employs someone specifically to monitor the content of the streaming broadcast and with the authority and capacity to prescreen that content (delayed posting), there could be greater liability on the part of the college or university.

Sun and McClellan (2019) explained that

> the legal definition of *harassment* varies by states, but those definitions generally describe unwelcomed, unwanted, and uninvited conduct (including speech) which is annoying, threatening, or intimidating ("Harassment law and legal definition," 2016). Higher education institutions which engage in policies or practices to prevent or address harassing behavior in a broad sense are generally on solid ground. However, when in an effort to advance

their institutional values of inclusion and respect these policies or practices begin to take the form of speech codes then they may run far greater risk of being seen by the courts The definition of as interfering with protected speech. (pp. 67–68)

Commercial Speech

Laws related to commercial speech may also inform how colleges and universities deal with speech related to certain aspects of esports programs. In *Central Hudson Gas & Electric Corp. v. Public Service Commission of New York* (1980), the court established a test for determining whether expressive behavior is commercial. The test asks four questions about the speech:

1. Does it concern an unlawful act, or is it misleading?
2. Is the government interest at hand substantial?
3. Does the regulation directly advance that governmental interest?
4. Is the regulation narrowly tailored to serve that interest? (Sun & McClellan, 2019, p. 80)

How might this come up in the context of collegiate esports? Imagine an esports club team that sells programs as part of its effort to fund the group's activities. The team provides space in the program to sponsors based on the amount of their support, and it also sells individual advertisements in the program. We will discuss the intersection of gambling and esports later in this chapter, but for our purposes here imagine that the club team receives an advertisement on a recurring basis from an online gambling entity. The institution is located in a state that expressly prohibits online gambling as well as gambling on sports. Alternatively, given the substantial number of males among the fans of the team, consider the possibility that the team secure sponsorship from an adult novelty and nude dancing emporium just outside the town where the school is located. It is a legal enterprise in the state, but it is not in keeping with the espoused values or brand image of the public institution. Court guidance in instances such as this one is unclear (Kaplin & Lee, 2013).

Internal or External Speech

Higher education institutions may only regulate internal speech, that which takes place in the context of its programs and service. They have no authority to regulate external speech. To be clear, the distinction between internal and external speech depends on the role in which the person or organization is engaging in expressive behavior—not the geography. Like the categories of exempted speech, the distinction between internal and external seems fairly straightforward. However, as with the challenges in recognizing whether particular speech falls into one of the exempted categories, the distinction is not always as clear as the dichotomous terminology seems to indicate. Consider this example: A group of people, including some student-athletes from the varsity esports team, comes together to play esports at an apartment off campus with members of a local community esports team. The competition also involves students and community members playing from various other locations. Comments are made in the game by one student to another that are perceived by the recipient as both offensive and intimidating. The aggrieved student decides to pursue the matter. They claim that the college's code of conduct, that specifically notes it covers behavior and speech in internal settings only, has been violated. If you received the complaint in your institutional role, would you see the institution as having jurisdiction? What if word of the party was circulated via the unofficial social media feed of the esports team, used for student-athletes to communicate with one another and to which at least one of the coaching staff (a recent graduate of the school and a former esports student-athlete) is subscribed? What if the athletic department offered participation points for esports team members who attended (points used to determine which of the teams in athletics is awarded various recognitions at the end-of-the-year sports banquet)? What if the person making the remarks was one of the cocaptains of the esports team and the one who had circulated the message via social media?

Alternatively, consider the possibility that a college has a high-profile esports student-athlete. As a prospective student, the recruit had a substantial and well-established fan base that subscribed to the person's stream. The individual was also engaged in several ongoing sponsorship deals that have been maintained throughout their time as a student-athlete for the college. The student-athlete continued to do very well in esports competitions for the school and also took part in tournaments outside of the intercollegiate context, permissible activity for members of the school's esports program. During one of these tournaments outside of the institutional context the student-athlete becomes involved in a very widely publicized outing of the sexual orientation of another player in the competition. The immediate result of that outing is a torrent of graphic, vile, and hateful homophobic comments directed toward the now outed individual. The speech took place in an external context, but given the link between the student-athlete and the institution, there is considerable negative attention being generated for the school.

Space for Speech

We have discussed types of speech and whether speech is internal or external to the institution. Speech may also take place within institutionally controlled spaces (or forums), and the nature of those spaces is important in understanding the degree to which expressive behavior within them may be regulated by the college or university. There are three types of forums in higher education: public, limited public, and private or nonforum (Lake, 2011). It is generally the case that the more open the forum, the more free the speech. A public forum is a space in which anyone is welcome to participate and where all forms of protected speech are free from content or viewpoint censorship. Reasonable time, place, and manner restrictions are possible for public forums. Limited public forums, sometimes referred to as designated forums, are made available by higher education institutions for specific purposes. "Viewpoint discrimination is not permissible in limited public forums, but content can be regulated if reasonable in light of the established purpose for the forum" (Sun & McClellan, 2019, p. 69). Some spaces are not generally open to the public and may be open to only some members of the institutional community. These are private or nonforums (Lake, 2011).

> In such places, the freedom of speech/association of the institution of higher education itself (or the student affairs administrator or other employee) may be at stake, and allowing forum analysis would squelch speech or association and/or the dedicated use of the property for a non-speech purpose. (Lake, 2011, p. 218)

Higher education institutions would be well advised to consider various forums of speech as they create and manage live events and streaming of events as part of their esports programs.

> The mantra of wide viewpoint access and reasonable regulation in light of the purposes of a forum should perpetually reverberate in . . . practice. The actual process of illuminating the educational and developmental nature and purposes of a forum is critical in any legal challenge to regulations under the First Amendment. (Lake, 2011, p. 213)

Digital Speech

Take a moment and imagine what it might be like if colleges and universities engaged in live streaming basketball or football games. As part of the live stream experience, visualize also that fans could post whatever messages they might wish to share, under whatever name they chose to use, their thoughts on the game. Welcome to the world of digital communication and esports.

Esports are, by their very nature, digital entities, and the communication and expression associated with esports activities are commonly digital in nature. Ben-Porath (2018) observed:

> The growing influence of digital communication, including social media, has given rise to competing interpretations about its role in democratic life. Some, like Habermas, have described the "disintegration of the public sphere," a sadly fragmented set of debates separated by filter bubbles and tribal domains. Others see digital communication as democratizing, and specifically as making space for a thoughtful attentive media where public intellectuals can profess their views to a reading audience, and where people of diverse backgrounds and worldviews can develop a following. (p. 2)

Expressive behavior taking place in digital spaces, speech that is computer mediated and that is conveyed via LANs or the internet, is a matter of still-evolving law.

> Much of that discussion, however, aligns itself with the idea laid out in *United States v. Alkhabaz aka Jake Baker* (1997) in which the court indicated computer-mediated communication might require some fine tuning of laws but does not change the basic analysis relative to First Amendment. (Sun & McClellan, 2019, p. 65)

Sun and McClellan (2019) cautioned,

> The way in which the intersection of higher education institutions' interests in both supporting free speech and inclusive campus communities plays out in digital communication environments is an exemplar of the truism: there are few things more certain than the uncertainty of what lies ahead. (p. 91)

Colleges and universities establishing or maintaining esports programs need not allow uncertainty to prevent them from taking responsible proactive measures related to ensuring those programs support both free speech and institutional values, including values of human dignity and inclusion. Kaplin et al. (2019) suggested treating student cyberspaces (e.g., web streams) like student publications. Avoid assuming responsibility for oversight and regulation where possible; students not acting as employees are not acting as agents of the institution and have the opportunity for enhanced learning and development through taking on these roles. Kaplin et al. (2019) also encouraged higher education institutions to work with campus constituents, particularly students, to develop a cyberspace code of ethics to be enforced by peer pressure and counterspeech. Institutions may also consider developing conflict resolution mechanisms related specifically to situations arising from digital communication.

Student-Athlete Speech

Some colleges and universities are inclined to monitor the digital communication of their student-athletes (Browning, 2012), and some contract with third-party vendors to do that work (Thamel, 2012). Such actions run the risk of raising both free speech and privacy issues. Following efforts by higher education institutions to require student-athletes to surrender the passwords to their social media accounts, a number of states passed legislation prohibiting the practice (Snyder et al., 2015; Thamel, 2012). The temptation to monitor student-athletes' social media might be particularly compelling to colleges and universities, given the extent to which these students engage in digital communication and the high profile that some of them have in cyberspace as esports athletes or media figures.

Sun and McClellan (2019) argued that the practice of monitoring student-athletes' social media content is unwise for two reasons. First, "It seems likely that any corrective or disciplinary action taken against a student on the basis of their online speech would open the program and the university to legal action related to restriction of free speech" (p. 104). Second,

> engaging in such monitoring brings with it an obligation to do so in consistent fashion. Failing that might lead to challenges from an athletics governance group . . . or in a court were there to be in [*sic*] instance in which a student-athlete came to harm or another person came to harm by a student-athlete where it could be argued that the program and institution could have or should have foreseen the potential for harm based on social media speech that it has a policy of monitoring. (Sun & McClellan, 2019, p. 104)

Protection of Minors

Esports and minors go together like red beans and rice. Kaplin et al. (2019) observed:

> Children may be on campus for at least three reasons: they are enrolled in campus educational, athletic, or social programs (such as summer camps); they are attending an event or using a campus facility, such as a day care center; or they are trespassers. (pp. 261–262)

However, as Alkire and Franke (2003) correctly pointed out to colleges and universities, "Your institution's interactions with children—and therefore, its liability—may also go farther afield than your campus. Faculty, staff, or students may be involved with children in off-campus programs through tutoring, student teaching, or community service activities" (p. 2). Alkire and Frank (2003) went on to add,

> The campus visits that concern us most are those in which parents are not present to supervise their children. Should harm come to minors then, educational institutions may be held liable. Even if parents are present, however, institutions may be held liable. (p. 2)

The Esports Integrity Coalition (2019a) described harm as "anything that adversely affects a child's physical or mental health, or intellectual, social, or behavioral development" (para. 7). They went on to specifically describe the following forms of harm:

> Sexual abuse—where a child is forced, persuaded or encouraged to take part in sexual activity, whether or not physical contact is involved (including grooming, where an individual seeks to befriend a child in order to take advantage of them for sexual purposes).
> Physical abuse—where physical harm is inflicted on a child, including injuries such as bruises, broken bones, burns or cuts [including through hazing].
> Emotional abuse—where a child is emotionally mistreated, which includes such things as bullying, or humiliating or scaring a child (this could include instances of trolling, flaming, and cyberbullying).
> Financial abuse—where a child is defrauded, exploited or otherwise placed under any financial pressure, including in the context of gambling. (para. 9)

It is not difficult to imagine that minors could be subjected to any of these forms of harm in the context of esports programming in higher education.

Higher education institutions with curricular or cocurricular offerings in esports can reasonably imagine engaging minors in one setting or another related to those offerings. Minors might be enrolled in special summer academic or esports camps. Minors might participate in recruiting visits to campus, or esports team members might visit their schools as part of outreach or community service. Minors might be engaging in online streaming chat or attending esports live events. Indeed, depending on the age of the student and the applicable laws of the state in which the college or university is located, some of the enrolled students involved in curricular or cocurricular esports offerings may be considered minors. Hence, institutions have a legal and an ethical obligation to help ensure that no harm comes to minors involved in esports programming or esports-related programming.

The chances are good that a college or university has already established a youth protection program, "policies and programs aimed to mitigate the risks posed to children participating in various activities on campus" (Chupak et al., 2019, p. 35). These youth protection programs commonly have two primary components: "measures to screen individuals who work with minors and efforts to monitor compliance with youth protection standards" (p. 35). Colleges and universities interested in offering curricular or cocurricular esports programs would do well to revisit their institution's youth protection program in light of the possible esports offerings. Is what is there applicable? Does it need to be adapted? Does it need to be expanded?

Give additional thought to the digital dimension of esports in reviewing extant policies and procedures. There are several federal statutes that address protecting children from sexual abuse and exploitation using computer-mediated communication (Kaplin et al., 2019). The Communications Decency Act of 1996 (CDA), enacted as Title V of the Telecommunications Act of 1996 (110 Stat. 56), makes it a criminal offense to knowingly transmit obscene materials of a person under the age of 18 or to a person under the age of 18. The CDA also makes it a crime to knowingly allow your computer infrastructure to be used for such transmission. Other laws related to digital communication and child protection include the Child Pornography Prevention Act of 1996 (18 U.S.C. §§ 2251 et seq.) and Child Online Protection Act (47 U.S.C. § 231) (Kaplin et al., 2019).

We have already suggested that colleges and universities not take on responsibility for moderating online streaming communication related to their esports programming. Similarly, we caution against an institution adding any additional filters related to filtering or monitoring content on their internet or internal networks beyond those already in place to support the typical function of the institution.

It is important both as a matter of proactive legal protection and fulfilling ethical obligations to be sure that parents and guardians are provided with clear communications regarding the policies and practices of the college or university related to protecting minors. Where possible, parents and guardians should be required to affirm in writing that they have received and understand the information shared with them and agree to have their minors involved with that understanding.

There is no substitute for good training. Take the time to be sure students, staff, and faculty understand the policies and practices related to protecting minors and the important role they play in helping ensure that harm does not come to children involved in programs at the institution.

One last bit of advice: Be sure that the curricular and cocurricular esports programs at your college or university hold the value that listening to young people is important and that young people know when something does not feel right to them, even when they may not be fully able to say what exactly is bothering them or why.

Gambling

Rose (1980) outlined three waves of gambling in the history of the United States, and McClellan and Winters (2006) identified a fourth wave taking place early in the 21st century. Nearly 15 years later, McClellan (2019) described an emerging fifth wave driven by the expansion of legalized sports wagering, popularity of fantasy sports, and the social phenomenon of esports. He explained,

> It now appears that our nation is poised to begin a fifth wave of gambling based on the recent spread of legalized sports wagering; the growth of esports and fantasy sports and the emergence of wagering on them (all pari-mutuel); and the seeming readiness of state governments to expand the legalization of Internet gambling. (p. 25)

There are a lot of people and a lot of money involved in esports, and McClellan (2019) wryly pointed out, "Where money and people flow, gambling is never far behind" (p. 28). Betting opportunities in esports include cash and skins (virtual items that can be traded or sold to other players and so have a value) wagered through a variety of activities including traditional sports-style, fantasy-style (creating salary cap leagues through which one can compete), jackpot lottery–style, and casino-style games (Legal Sports Report, 2018). It is estimated that by 2020 15 million people will be placing wagers on esports with a value of roughly $30 billion (Heitner, 2016).

The legal status of gambling varies from state to state. Colleges and universities should be aware of the status of the legalization of sports wagering in their state and whether or not the state considers esports to be a form of sports on which wagering is permitted. It is also important to be mindful that, even though gambling is becoming legalized in more and more states, people may still decide to gamble outside legal channels for several reasons. They may find it more convenient to deal with a local bookie or bet online. They may not have the cash on hand (required to wager legally) but are willing to gamble on credit (illegal books typically do not require cash up front). Finally, and perhaps most significantly for higher education, they may not be of legal age to gamble in their state.

The association of gambling with esports brings with it the need for vigilance related to the integrity of the contests and the reputation of higher education institutions. It also raises questions about potential health implications for players and fans. There is some evidence of a small to moderate positive relationship between esports participation and gambling on online gaming, online gambling, and problem gambling (Macey & Humari, 2018).

Colleges and universities could include information on compliance, legal, and health issues related to esports gambling available in their educational programs for student-athletes, students at large, and staff and faculty (particularly those associated with the esports program). The inclusion of such language in codes of conduct is particularly important in light of the fact that the NCAA, which has detailed policies regarding gambling and an outstanding gambling education program, appears poised to maintain its distance from esports, and neither the NAIA nor the NJCAA have policies regarding gambling. It may also be helpful to specifically address gambling in codes of conduct for student-athletes and for students across campus. Students may not connect generic references prohibiting illegal conduct with gambling behavior, given how ubiquitous such behavior is in our society.

Student-Athlete Health

Problem and pathological gambling is an example of a student health concern in esports. There are others. Although some may have trouble imagining how someone can be injured as a result of playing games online, the evidence of such injuries is clear. DiFrancisco-Donoghue et al. (2019) surveyed 65 intercollegiate varsity esports athletes in Canada and the United States regarding their experience with injuries. The most frequently reported complaints were eye fatigue (56%), neck and back pain (42%), wrist pain (36%), and hand pain (32%). However, only 2% of the student-athletes responding to the survey had sought medical attention. Thomas Andre, a faculty member in health, exercise science, and recreation management at the University of Mississippi and an esports player, observed changes in his own health as his time playing increased. "I started noticing

. . . poor sleep, elevated heart rate; I could feel myself not blinking as much, my breathing would get shallow" (quoted in Gabler, 2019, para. 4). These observations spurred him to begin studying the health of esports players at his university.

> The results showed that, while gaming, players had similar accelerated heart rates and recovery periods as competitive athletes during exercise. . . . These guys are only playing for maybe 30 minutes and the peak heart rate is like doing a max test. (paras. 5–6)

Hand and wrist injuries should come as no surprise given the rapid repetitive motions that characterize esports. Doran (2017) reported that the typical competitive player will take 300 actions per minute in an esports game, and elite players may take 400 to 500 actions per minute. Eye strain comes as no surprise given that esports athletes are staring (and trying not to blink) at computer screens for hours and hours on end while tracking rapidly developing movements with their eyes. Back and neck strain as well as elevated heart rates are understandable as a consequence of the stress these student-athletes undergo during competition. These injuries, particularly left unaddressed over time, can lead to diminished performance, missed games, or the end of competitive play (Bräutigam, 2016).

We are still in the relatively early days of the mass popularity of esports, and our understanding of the toll it can take on the health of athletes competing in the sport is developing. As one esports industry professional said, "This is like football in the days of leather helmets" (Brasch, 2019, para. 11). There are, however, developments in equipment, facilities design, nutrition, sports medicine, and training that can all contribute to helping college and university esports student-athletes be healthier. Recalling from chapter 1 that some in higher education see esports as an inexpensive way to pursue various institutional goals, we need to be clear that the health of student-athletes is no place to try to get in the game on the cheap.

DiFrancisco-Donoghue et al. (2019) asserted,

> Working with any sport team at any level requires a relationship with the players and the coach. A plan of services should include baseline testing, clinical evaluations and services as well as physical and mental health assessments. This can help with academic performance and social behaviours and should be presented in a way that does not bombard the players with too many evaluations or tests but offers a time frame and an explanation of how these tests can benefit them. (para. 15)

They offer a model, shown in Figure 5.2, for training and medical support of esports athletes that could inform the efforts of higher education institutions determined to take their obligations in this area seriously.

Governance

The rapid adoption of esports in higher education since the turn of the 21st century is sometimes described in terms like *uncharted territory, wild west,* or *new frontier*—all commonly associated with the westward expansion of the United States (Bauer-Wolf, 2019; Lumb, 2018; Nguyen, 2019). These descriptive phrases reflect both the rapidity of change and the absence of unified governance that have characterized this adoption.

The absence of governance in esports presents significant ethical and legal peril, particularly in regard to intercollegiate varsity programs. Consider as an example the question of recruiting. Ethical practices in recruiting students based on the availability of an RSO, club team, or curricular offering in esports can reasonably be understood to be the same as those established for the general recruitment of students in higher education. Enrollment professionals in colleges and universities promulgate these standards through decisions made in the field's well-established professional associations, most notably as described in the National Association of College Admission Counseling's (2018) *Code of Ethics and Professional Practices*. Still, despite the presence of a substantive governance infrastructure, scandals in college recruitment and admissions make headlines (Quintana, 2019; Yan, 2019). The ethical standards and practices related to recruiting intercollegiate varsity student-athletes are addressed through the intercollegiate athletics association of which the institution is a member (NAIA, NCAA, or NJCAA). However, none of these associations currently recognizes esports as a form of sport. So who is the governing entity for intercollegiate varsity esports? The answer as of 2019 has been no one. That is disconcerting at best.

Who might step in to fill this void? The three major intercollegiate athletics associations all appear reluctant to do so. Although no doubt attracted by the level of activity and the amount of money associated with esports, these traditional associations may yet be skeptical of the degree to which esports fits their brand image, wary of their ability to navigate the challenging question of ownership of the games that serve as the basis for esports competition, and uncertain about how to handle issues of amateurism (a cherished value in intercollegiate athletics) in esports. Tespa's strength is in the area of RSOs and club team esports programs. NACE, whose membership includes over 90% of the colleges and universities with extant intercollegiate varsity

Figure 5.2. Model for esports athlete medical support.

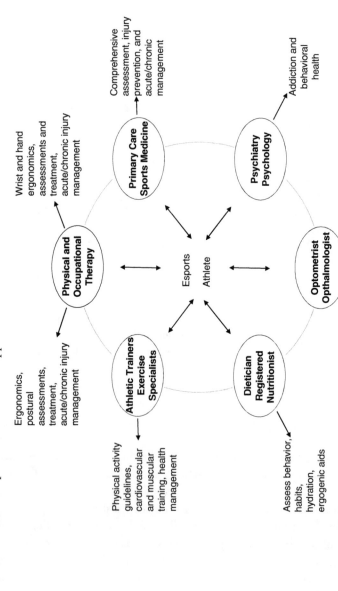

Note. Adapted from DiFrancisco-Donoghue et al. (2019).

esports programs (Bauer-Wolf, 2019), seems the likely candidate to fill this role.

The NACE 2019 convention, its second, may have marked an important turning point in NACE stepping forward to become the prevailing governance body of intercollegiate varsity esports. The member institutions at the meeting ratified bylaws and a constitution for the organization (National Association of Collegiate Esports, 2019c). Taken together these documents addressed critically important issues including recruitment, eligibility, and financial support for student-athletes. Highlights of the NACE policies for each of these issues are outlined in the following paragraphs.

New student recruiting may begin September 1 of each year, and transfer recruiting may begin February 1 (National Association of Collegiate Esports, 2019c). The student-athletes sign an Intent to Compete form, binding the student-athlete and institution for one year. That agreement must be renewed annually in order to remain valid. NACE will serve as a repository for all of the Intent to Compete forms. A potential esports student-athlete is free to speak with any member institution until they have signed an Intent to Compete form. With regard to student-athletes who might transfer, member institutions may not contact them until their Intent to Commit form has expired.

Student-athletes must be enrolled on a full-time basis in order to be eligible to compete (National Association of Collegiate Esports, 2019c). NACE does not stipulate any initial or continuing academic eligibility requirements; each member institution determines academic eligibility for its student-athletes. Although this may provide greater flexibility at the local level, it seems to increase opportunities for conflicts to arise between the interests of academic integrity and rigor and interests of fielding the most competitive team. The policy could also lead to a race to the bottom with regard to academic standards.

NACE states that the financial aid awarded to an esports student-athlete cannot exceed the combined value of tuition, fees, books, room, and board (National Association of Collegiate Esports, 2019c). NACE's other policies with regard to financial support for esports student-athletes mark a significant departure from extant policies of major higher education collegiate athletics associations, reflecting a philosophical and operational departure from the idea of amateurism (more on this in chapter 6). NACE places no restrictions on the amount a student-athlete can earn from esports activities outside of those of their institution, and NACE allows member institutions to determine how they will allocate prize monies won by their student-athletes in playing for their college or university. Further, there are no restrictions on expenses (including reimbursements to student-athletes) incurred by the institution for expenditures related to intercollegiate competition. There are also no restrictions on expenses (including reimbursements) related to the student-athlete members on the team (team-building trips, mission trips, etc.). Although these policies are an understandable approach given the nature of esports and the reality that many student-athletes begin earning money through their involvement well before they are being recruited by colleges and universities, this seems like a situation fraught with opportunities for creating unfair advantages and undue influence.

Conclusion

Several times throughout this chapter and throughout this book we have highlighted dimensions of esports that may present conflicts with the institutional values (including ethical and principled conduct, compliance with the law, and shared governance) of some colleges and universities. Games that glorify fighting or conquest, lack of civility and presence of homophobia or misogyny, association with gambling (legal or otherwise), and departure from the model of amateurism are just some of those dimensions.

The dilemma of how to reconcile some elements of esports with institutional values is an ill-formed problem, but it is not unresolvable. Resolving it requires that colleges and universities interested in offering esports programming begin by revisiting and reaffirming their values relative to curricular and cocurricular programming and then identify esports pathways that are consistent with those values. It will be insufficient, however, to take a "one and done" approach to these deliberations. The process of revisiting and reaffirming values, monitoring changes in available esports options, and assessing the degree to which espoused intentions match enacted decisions ought to be ongoing. The journey of initial institutional consideration and ongoing assessment and reflection presents valuable opportunities for inclusive shared governance as well as for learning and development.

6

SUMMING UP AND LOOKING FORWARD

The Danish physicist Niels Bohr is often credited for having commented, "It is difficult to make predictions, especially about the future" (Quote Investigator, 2013). The accuracy of the attribution is in question, but the observation itself merits attention. Mindful of apocryphal admonition, we will use this final chapter to highlight important themes and recommendations from earlier chapters and to identify challenges and opportunities that may lie ahead for higher education institutions offering students curricular or cocurricular esports programming.

Highlighted Themes and Recommendations

This section highlights a number of important themes woven throughout the preceding chapters, both as a reminder to readers and to inform consideration of the future challenges and opportunities that are discussed later in the chapter.

Esports is exciting, flashy, wildly popular, and rapidly changing. Higher education is none of those things. So how can we bring the two together in ways that hold some promise for a successful venture? One essential strategy is to root the innovative esports effort in institutional mission, values, ethics, and legal principles that are relatively constant. Let these serve as the foundation on which curricular and cocurricular esports offerings are considered and brought forward.

That said, a second important strategy is do not simply try to force this relatively new form of competition, education, and entertainment into an old box. Although not completely without precedent, esports in higher education is unique in many ways. We will be well advised to allow ourselves to be made somewhat uncomfortable by new organizational models, competition and communication structures, and cross-cutting curricular and cocurricular offerings. The willingness to engage in informed risk-taking may lead to greater success for the esports programs and the institution and may offer lessons that can be brought to bear on other areas of endeavor.

Third, be clear about institutional purposes for engaging in esports. What goals are your institution pursuing through its esports programs? Whatever those goals may be, there should be a clear connection between them and the core mission of your college or university.

The point has been made throughout this book that there will be esports competitors and fans across a variety of levels of interest and skill in any student body. It is for this reason that we have encouraged schools to, fourth, offer the fullest suite possible of curricular and cocurricular programs for their situation. The curricular realm could include stand-alone academic presentations (including sessions on career opportunities related to esports), noncredit-bearing courses, certificates, and minors and majors leading to degrees. The cocurriculum includes the three primary forms of RSO, club team, and varsity sport, but it is also important to be cognizant of those groups of students on the campus who are involved in esports outside the structured offerings of the school.

Fifth, the most fully realized esports programs in higher education will be those in which the curricular and cocurricular offerings are meaningfully related to one another. This will help promote the greatest opportunities for learning and development and help ensure that the esports programs are not isolated from the rest of campus life simply because they are new or different.

Higher education is not noted for its agility or rapidity of action. On the contrary, colleges and universities have developed very deliberative processes for consideration of questions of interest to the campus community. Esports, however, is a rapidly evolving field. Sixth, colleges and universities wishing to engage in esports programs need to move quickly but thoughtfully to organize their efforts (perhaps in cross-divisional leadership groups) in ways that are scaled for their institution.

Seventh, appropriate levels of investment of resources (including funds, space, and labor) are important to consider. As noted in chapter 1, some schools see esports as an inexpensive way to increase enrollments or pursue other goals. Overinvestment can lead to waste while denying badly needed resources for other areas and creating resentment toward the esports programs. Underinvestment can have equally unpleasant consequences that result in students being underserved and the college or university being poorly represented.

Creating and monitoring the budgets related to esports programs are, therefore, areas that ought to get considerable attention in planning and management. Barr and McClellan (2018) offered a number of very helpful tips for budget managers, including noting the tendency for people to overestimate potential revenue and underestimate expenses. They also cautioned that care needs to be given in discerning and clearly articulating any hidden and recurring costs associated with programs.

Networking can also be important to success in the area of esports. The eighth theme is to find other colleges and universities in your area that are engaged in or considering esports, particularly those similar to your school, and share information and resources with one another. Explore opportunities for both cooperation and competition.

The ninth theme throughout this book is that students are way ahead of faculty or staff when it comes to esports. We believe that students should always be included in the shared governance of colleges and universities, but we believe that when it comes to esports students can and should play an important role in informing, guiding, and (in some instances, particularly in the cocurriculum) leading esports programs. Students engaged in this way are more likely to be retained, feel more satisfied with their experience, and learn more deeply. Institutions are more likely to develop programs with strong student support, greater viability, and enhanced competitive success.

Challenges Ahead

We acknowledge significant potential to support student and institutional success through esports programming at colleges and universities, but we are equally certain there are challenges ahead for esports in higher education. Among them are competition structure, competition climate, child protection, cheating, gambling, lack of reliable relevant data to inform decisions, and the advent of an esports arms race. Each of these is discussed in this section.

Competition Structure

An immediate challenge facing club teams and varsity teams in intercollegiate esports is the problem of establishing competition structures. Efforts need to be made to set up ongoing leagues and associated championship structures, particularly in light of the likely continued resistance on the part of the NCAA to embrace esports. Tips for engaging in this work were shared in chapters 2 and 3.

Competition Climate

Issues of diversity, civility, respect, and inclusion are at the forefront of many discussions at higher education institutions across the United States. Esports programs are very likely to be a new locus of attention for such conversations. We spoke in chapter 5 of the ethical and legal problems that colleges and universities could face as a result of the homophobia, misogyny, and racism that are too often a part of esports culture. It bears repeating that failing to address the climate issues presents a threat to almost any goal one could imagine a college or university having as a result of its decision to engage in esports programming.

Many colleges and universities have aspirational statements regarding diversity and inclusion, promotion of academic freedom, and protection of free speech. These institutions also have policies and procedures to address situations in which members of the community feel there has been some transgression of these values. It would be helpful for colleges and universities wishing to engage in esports programing to ensure their statements, policies, and procedures are clearly inclusive of digital communication and to consider the ways in which the student, faculty, and staff leadership of the campus community can engage in proactive efforts to foster more respectful and inclusive campus conversations.

Child Protection

The Esports Integrity Coalition (ESIC) is a not-for-profit organization established to help prevent, detect, and address cheating in esports (Esports Integrity Coalition, 2019b). ESIC is also concerned with child protection in esports (Esports Integrity Coalition, 2019a). Keeping in mind the legal status of many college students as well as the great likelihood that esports players involved in college activities could interact with minors involved in competitions either as players or as fans (and the considerable attention given to the responsibility of colleges and universities to protect minors on their campus or involved in their programs and services), this is a topic that ought to get attention from higher education institutions involved in esports programming.

This is such a new and evolving area of practice that it is difficult for us to do much more than simply raise the issue for consideration and attention. Higher education might also press NACE and other associations to convene conversations on how higher education might collectively and proactively engage this challenge.

Cheating

Cheating is a problem and a threat in professional esports. Game publishers, tournament and league organizers, sponsors, team owners, and athletes alike do not want cheating involved in the sport (Ashton, 2019). Even the legal gambling industry's interest in esports is threatened.

There is every reason to believe that cheating will emerge as a challenge for esports in higher education. A great deal of money and prestige are involved in college esports, and more of each is on the way. College student-athletes are particularly vulnerable to exploitation and manipulation by those involved in illegal gambling activities (McClellan et al., 2006). In addition, college students are in the process of developing their cognitive and moral identities. The combination seems fraught with problematic potential.

ESIC is an organization with members including esports publishers, tournament organizers, leagues, and others. ESIC divides esports cheating into two primary forms—cheating in order to gain a competitive advantage and match-fixing in order to gain through payoffs or gambling (Esports Integrity Coalition, 2016). The former, cheating to win, includes software cheats and hacks, online attacks, doping, and disabling or abusing opponents (physically inhibiting their performance). The latter includes match-fixing (deliberately underperforming in a match in order to lose), corrupting officials and technicians, spot-fixing (deliberately underperforming in part of a match either to lose or to keep certain statistics low), and manipulating tournament structures (deliberately underperforming in a match so as to take advantage of a tournament structure such that one ends up with a clearer path to the championship). In rank order of threat to esports based on likelihood and potential impact of occurence, ESIC lists software cheats, online attacks to slow or disable an opponent, match-fixing, and doping as the most significant forms of cheating threats to esports.

There are a number of ways that cheating in esports can be detected. These include monitoring player equipment and competition hardware and networks, real-time monitoring by officials as well as competitors and fans, and reviewing competitions (Ashton, 2019). The Valve Anti-Cheat System (VACS), which was developed to scan user computers for installed software hacks that would allow for cheating, is one example of the development of technological monitoring techniques to detect cheating in esports (Ashton, 2019).

Higher education institutions involved in esports, either directly or through their leagues or associations, could consider becoming members of ESIC. They might also invest in education materials addressing cheating in esports, including cheating across the full spectrum of competitive play. Colleges and universities could also include statements on cheating in their esports policies, develop protocols for addressing suspected instances of cheating, and invest in affordable cheating prevention and detection technologies for their esports programs.

Gambling

It should come as no surprise that where significant public interest and substantial sums of money are involved in a competitive sporting enterprise, those interested in engaging in or promoting gambling on that activity are not far behind. It has been estimated that worldwide revenue from gambling on esports in 2014 was $24 million, and by 2020 it is projected that figure will grow to $1.8 billion (Statista, 2015). Indeed, McClellan (2019) argued that esports is among the causes of what he described as the growing fifth wave of gambling in the United States.

Student gambling and gambling on intercollegiate athletics are nothing new in higher education (McClellan et al., 2006). Recent changes in federal law as well as the growth of fantasy sports and esports are fueling increased gambling activity in the United States, and college students are likely to be engaged (either legally or illegally) in esports gambling just as they are in other forms of gambling, including sports gambling (McClellan, 2019).

Gambling can be a factor contributing to the popularity of a given sport, but it can only be a positive factor if those engaged in wagering believe that the contests are free of undue influence on the outcome (i.e., *fixing*). ESIC expressed confidence that the esports industry deals with cheating to gain a competitive edge pretty well, but they argue that match- or spot-fixing is not being thoroughly addressed. "There is little understanding of betting [on esports] and how betting fraud drives match-fixing and rules and regulations are cursory where they exist at all" (Esports Integrity Coalition, 2016, p. 9).

The NCAA opposes gambling on intercollegiate athletics, and it has policies in place reflecting that position. It has an infrastructure for educating student-athletes, coaches, and others about the risks associated with gambling on college sports and gambling by student-athletes, and it has active and arguably effective monitoring mechanisms in place. Neither the NAIA nor the NJCAA have such policies. Given the potential harm to student-athletes and institutions that could come about as the result of improper gambling activities related to esports, it seems that member institutions of NAIA and the NJCAA (associations that have engaged with esports in higher education) might encourage those organizations to reconsider their hands-off approach to gambling issues.

Colleges and universities with cocurricular esports programs ought to consider providing students, club advisers, coaches, and others with information on college student gambling and encourage students to report any concerns they have about gambling on any activity to the institution. Members of NACE and Tespa should encourage those groups to help support proactive development and implementation of education programs and policies related to gambling in esports. In addition, as noted earlier, colleges and universities may find it helpful to become members of ESIC and take advantage of the resources available through that organization.

Lack of Reliable Relevant Data

Considering the formative nature of esports programming in higher education, there is an urgent need for data across a wide variety of topics. However, the absence of readily available relevant data and the challenges associated with collecting data given the current diffusion of higher education efforts in esports present substantial challenges to addressing that need. The challenge is even more acute given the rapidly changing nature of esports in higher education.

Colleges and universities can provide tremendous leadership in this area through encouraging assessment and research by their own faculty and staff and participating in studies being conducted by colleagues at other institutions or reputable associations and organizations. Colleges and universities can also work to ensure that those involved in their esports programming have access to the latest information available on esports and are encouraged to consider how such information might help inform curricular and cocurricular offerings.

Esports Arms Race

Escalating expenditures for intercollegiate athletics as a consequence of efforts to be competitive, sometimes referred to as an *arms race*, are a subject of concern among a variety of higher education constituents. There is nothing new about the arms race in athletic facilities (McNair, 2019), though the scope of the facilities through which the race is being enacted has broadened beyond the actual competitive arenas to include spaces for administrative support, training, academic support of student-athletes, residential areas, and more. More recently, in addition to discussion of facilities, there has been attention given to growing numbers of administrative and professional staff (Carlton, 2017) and the salaries of coaches (Tsitsos & Nixon, 2012). The considerable attention given to the arms race in intercollegiate athletics, however, seems to have done little to impede new investments. Perhaps this is because, as Big 12 commissioner Bob Bowlsby once observed, "The only thing worse than being in the arms race is not being in the arms race, because you fall behind and you don't have the tools that you need to get the job done" (quoted in Redd, 2018, para. 8).

It seems probable that the intercollegiate arms race will manifest itself among colleges and universities hosting varsity esports programs. Hennen (2019) pointed to early evidence that the race, or at least the qualifying heats, has already begun. It did not take long for people to begin developing lists of the best esports facilities in higher education (see Liu, 2019, as an example of such a list), and some institutions have begun charging fees to support the operation and expansion of their esports facilities (Stoller, 2019).

Bowen (1980) powerfully argued that higher education institutions, in the pursuit of prestige, will spend every dollar they can raise. The arms race in intercollegiate athletics provides support for Bowen's argument. Sadly, we see it as likely that Bowen's theory will play itself out in esports in higher education as well. We wish that we had powerful advice to offer, but the truth is that all we have is a cautionary note. Colleges and universities should take some time to figure out which investments will truly contribute to their desired goals—whatever they may be. Do not rush to build spaces or buy equipment that will not suit the needs of students in just a few short years. Better to set a steady pace early in this race and finish strong rather than burn out early and be an also-ran.

Opportunities Ahead

Just as we looked ahead to the challenges presented to higher education by the development of esports programming, we look forward in this section to the opportunities that esports programs could afford. Some of the things that are challenges are also opportunities. Competition structure and governance, competition and campus cultures, and reliable data are examples. Other opportunities described here include student recruitment and success networks with high schools, partnerships with the esports industry, and amateurism.

Competition Structure and Governance

It has been pointed out throughout this book that the systems of competition structures and governance for collegiate cocurricular esports programs are in their infancy. There is an opportunity available for colleges and universities to create those systems in ways that are responsive to their needs, supportive of students involved as casual participants or athletes, and consistent with important educational and institutional values.

Both Tespa and NACE are relatively young organizations, and it is our impression they are doing important early work in developing competition structures and governance mechanisms. Colleges and universities could contribute to that work through membership and active engagements. The alternative is to begin anew and work collectively to develop alternative channels for fostering systems of competition structures and governance, but it would be important in doing so to have a clear shared understanding of what those institutions involved in such an effort would expect from a new organization that is not currently available from either Tespa or NACE or that could not be brought about through exerting influence within those two bodies.

It seems unlikely that the NCAA will embrace esports in the near future, but both the NAIA and the NJCAA are already involved. Member institutions of both associations have varsity esports teams, and there are opportunities within those two sports associations to shape competitive structures and governance as well.

Competition and Campus Cultures

It is precisely because the competition culture in esports can be so challenging in regard to diversity and inclusion that there is an opportunity here as well. Colleges and universities cannot simply ignore the issue; they are compelled to engage it if they are going to offer curricular and cocurricular esports programming.

Ensuring inclusive and respectful competition climates begins with recruiting coaches, program staff, and athletes. Clearly articulating the values of the program, showcasing adherence efforts, and contributing to a welcoming environment as part of the selection process all combine as an important early step.

Intercollegiate esports programs also have an opportunity to help shape the competition culture through the choices they make regarding the games in which they will participate. As noted in chapter 5, some game publishers are recognized for their work in creating more inclusive games. Supporting their efforts could be a positive step forward. So too could be advocating with competition and governance structures to insist that the choice of games for which competitions are sponsored includes consideration of the degree to which games promote inclusion and respect.

Sharing information with student-athletes about what does and does not contribute to in-game performance is another promising strategy to impact competition culture. This provides an opportunity to highlight issues of health as well as inclusion.

As noted earlier in the book, the best esports programs are those that connect curricular and cocurricular elements. That is true of efforts to promote inclusive and respectful competitive cultures as well. Esports programs can look to faculty on campus with experience and expertise in matters of inclusion, communication, and organizational culture as advocates, advisers, and consultants for the effort.

A diverse and inclusive esports program can serve as a model and center of energy for fostering the same qualities in the broader campus community. It can help draw a more diverse group of students to campus, either as participants or as fans, and encourage shared learning and esprit de corps.

Reliable Data

We discussed the challenges presented by the lack of reliable and relevant data on esports in higher education earlier in this section. Esports also presents a tremendous opportunity for assessment and research (Wagner, n.d.). Both traditional scholarship and the scholarship of practice are needed, and there are ample opportunities across a variety of academic and professional domains—psychology, sociology, physiology, sports management, sports medicine, business, and more.

Qualitative inquiries should be a part of the effort to bring data forward. There are important questions to be addressed that are best explored through qualitative studies. How do student-athletes incorporate esports as an element of their identity? What are the experiences of student-athletes in intercollegiate varsity competition? What pathways are people taking to become esports advisers and coaches, and how do they see themselves moving forward in the field? What strategies are student-athletes in esports who are subjected to online harassment using to work through that behavior? These are just a few examples of interesting lines of qualitative inquiry for esports in higher education.

Student Recruitment and Success Networks

Chapter 1 described the growth of esports as part of the offerings available to students in both high school and higher education. This shared activity can provide an opportunity to build new student recruitment and student success networks. The collaboration between Riverside School District in Pennsylvania and Lackawanna College (Bolus, 2019) is one example of this sort of partnership. One can imagine early recruitment, peer mentoring, student coaching, competition climate, joint facilities, coappointment of coaches, and shared fundraising and friend-making among the possible areas where esports could serve as a focal point around which high schools and higher education institutions might work closely together. Achieving the full potential benefit of these opportunities will require the thoughtful, purposeful, and persistent cooperation of stakeholders in both the high schools and the colleges and universities just as with any other collaboration between secondary and postsecondary education.

Partnerships With Esports Industry

Another area of opportunity for colleges and universities involved in curricular and cocurricular esports programs is partnerships with the esports industry. Sponsorships supporting facilities, equipment, tournaments, and other programmatic needs for competition come quickly to mind, but sponsorships might also extend to support for academic offerings like certificate programs, symposia, or conferences. There could also be collaboration around shared research agendas. Students might find internship and employment opportunities in a wide array of esports-related professional roles, including, for example, game design, marketing, digital broadcasting, or event management. Although it might go without saying, it is important that all parties involved in partnerships between for-profit corporate interests and not-for-profit educational interests have a clear and complete understanding of one another's expectations and the ethics and values that must inform any activities born of the collaboration.

Amateurism

A final opportunity we want to point out is that the rise of esports, coupled with other developments (including legal decisions regarding players' rights to their image and the effort of some states to pass legislation affirming those rights for players), presents an opportunity for higher education to reconsider amateurism as an essential element of intercollegiate athletics. Our point in raising this issue is not to advocate for one particular position or another; our goal in doing so is simply to point out that there is real opportunity here for discussion about what we want to build—whatever the outcome.

Of course, the purity of amateurism as we know it in American higher education today is a bit spurious in any case. Intercollegiate athletic associations permit international student-athletes to have competed for cash prizes outside our national boundaries, and student-athletes competing in the

Olympics who medal in their sport are permitted to accept the cash awards that come with those honors.

The role of amateurism in intercollegiate athletics is, as a practical matter, of greatest concern in a limited number of sports at particular types of institutions. Specifically, issues of amateurism are most associated with men's basketball and football in those conferences where substantial revenue is generated through the programs (including revenues from broadcasting licenses). One can hope, as do the authors, that we will see the day when women's sports command similar attention. Perhaps the success of women's soccer is a step in that direction.

Esports is not the first sport for which traditional notions of amateurism seem impractical in college and university athletics. Rodeo and bass fishing are two earlier examples that come quickly to mind. All three are activities in which potential student-athletes may well have engaged prior to being recruited at college in ways that would obviate them being classified as pure amateurs in the traditional sense of the word. They might have garnered sponsorships, earned cash prizes, or (at least in the case of esports) generated revenue through streaming.

NACE, which has emerged as a membership-based governance group for colleges and universities with varsity esports programs, has essentially walked away from the issue of amateurism in its initial set of bylaws and policies related to competition. We have a sense that the decision reflects both the practical realities of esports as it has developed and the limitations of a nascent governance group with limited resources to handle matters of enforcement even if it were so inclined. It remains to be seen whether colleges and universities will continue to support this hands-off approach as membership grows (or other governance options emerge).

Conclusion

Esports has undergone tremendous growth over the past decade or so. It sometimes seems like esports is everywhere we turn. It can be helpful as a matter of perspective to keep in mind that, despite its substantial popularity, 75% of Americans neither watch nor play esports (Ingraham, 2018). Where will it go from here? We suspect esports may not grow at the rate suggested by its biggest proponents. Some are already sounding a cautionary note about the hype, results, and sustainability of esports (D'Anastasio, 2019). However, we agree with Hennen (2019) that esports is likely to continue to be a large social phenomenon.

Esports is now a part of the curricular or cocurricular offerings of hundreds and hundreds of colleges and universities, and we believe that it will continue to be a part of campus life for many. Our hope is that the information shared in this book leaves our readers with the sense that there is so much that could happen—both good and bad—as a result of colleges and universities offering esports programs. We also hope that we have made the case that the degree to which those programs foster the success of students and institutions will be shaped largely by the extent to which students, staff, and faculty proactively and thoughtfully engage in the development and management of those programs. In that regard, there is nothing truly new about esports. So we close the book where we began. GLHF!

GLOSSARY

Aimbot: Software used in shooting games that allows for automatic targeting and firing, sometimes used to cheat

American Collegiate Esports League (ACEL): A not-for-profit organization that helps colleges and universities find opportunities to compete in esports conferences, leagues, and tournaments

Caster: An individual or organization that creates esports content for online streaming

Channel: A dedicated forum for streamed content, typically based in an online website such as YouTube

Club teams: Student organizations recognized by their college or university that compete in a particular sport with teams from other higher education institutions or from the community

Collegiate Starleague (CSL): A for-profit company (claiming to be the first esports collegiate gaming organization) that organizes esports competitions, including tournaments and leagues

Console: An electronic device on which video games may be played (as opposed to playing them on an arcade machine or on a computer)

Deviant play: Play or conduct that is outside the design of the game and social norms, often associated with harassing or hateful behavior or speech

Doping: Taking performance-enhancing drugs to improve competitive performance, sometimes a form of cheating

Esports: Multiplayer video games which are played competitively, often for spectators, either over local area networks (LAN) or online

Esports arena: A facility constructed or adapted specifically for the purpose of hosting esports competitions attended by spectators and that may also include facilities for team operation and support

Esports Integrity Coalition (ESIC): A not-for-profit membership organization that works to prevent, detect, and respond to cheating in esports, as well as to address matters of child protection in esports

Experience economy: An emerging economy driven by people interested in taking part in and sharing experiences, including esports as an example (Pine & Gilmore, 1998)

Fighting games: A genre of esports in which player avatars engage in physical combat

First-person shooter games (FPS): A genre of esports in which players take the first-person perspective of their character and engage in armed conflict with various types of guns or other weapons

Flaming: Posting insulting or offensive messages online

Freemium model: Esports games (or any good or service) made available at a core level for free but on which players pay for advanced-level features

Gaming computer: A computer configured to optimize gaming experience and performance

Gaymer: A term coined by LGBTQ members of the online gaming community to refer to themselves

GLHF!: A salutation shared at the beginning of an online game meaning "Good luck, and have fun!"

Intercollegiate varsity sports: Sports teams organized and managed by higher education institutions that compete with teams from other colleges and universities and for which student-athletes may receive athletic scholarships

League of Legends (LoL): One of the most popular esports games, a multiplayer online battle arena game (MOBA) published by Riot and made available through a freemium model

League of Legends Championship Series (LCS): The top esports professional league in North America

Local area network (LAN): A network connecting computers within a building or across a group of buildings

Match-fixing: Deliberately underperforming in a match in order to lose for the purpose of monetary gain through payoff or gambling

Multiplayer online battle arena games (MOBA): A genre of esports in which players engage as members of a team in battle competition with one or more other teams

National Association of Collegiate Esports (NACE): A nonprofit organization that serves to promote intercollegiate varsity esports through information sharing, organization of competitions, and governance

National Collegiate eSports Association (NCeSPA): A seemingly dormant company that sought to unify governance of esports in higher education and helped present competition opportunities

Nintendo 64: First sold in 1996, a popular game console manufactured by Nintendo, an early leader in home electronic gaming

Overwatch: Multiplayer team-based FPS game published by Blizzard Entertainment

Overwatch University League: A now defunct group that organized Overwatch tournaments for college students and college teams

Priming: The display of messages encouraging positive and inclusive play while games are loading

Real-time strategy games (RTS): A genre of esports in which individual players compete for control of a map through acquisition of resources and locations; precursors to MOBA games

Recognized/registered student organization (RSO): A campus student group that has been recognized by its college or university and to which privileges and responsibilities have been extended as a function of recognition/registration

Shoutcaster: An esports commentator or celebrity who (not in their role as player) creates content for streaming

Spot-fixing: Deliberately underperforming in a part of a match in order to lose or keep certain statistics low for the purpose of monetary gain through payoff or gambling

Streaming: An online form of broadcasting popular for esports competitions and other esports content

Student League for Intercollegiate Esports (SLICE): A for-profit company that organizes esports competitions, including tournaments and leagues

Sports and racing: A genre of esports in which players compete in sports or racing such as football, soccer, or motocross

Swatting: The criminal behavior of misleading emergency services or law enforcement personnel to respond to a false report of criminal or dangerous behavior in progress

Tespa: A nonprofit organization that promotes RSO and club team esports in colleges and universities through sharing information, supporting formation of leagues, and organizing competitions

Third-person shooter games (TPS): A genre of esports in which players compete from a third-person perspective using guns or other weapons

Tournament structure manipulation: Deliberately underperforming in a match in order to lose for the purpose of getting to a better path to the championship

Trolling: Posting comments online with the intent of causing commotion or disagreement

Twitch: One of the major platforms (along with YouTube) for streaming esports content

Valve Anti-Cheat System (VACS): A means to scan user computers for installed software hacks that would allow for cheating

Wallhack: Software that makes walls in a game either transparent or non-solid, sometimes used to cheat

Xbox: A video gaming brand from Microsoft that includes consoles, games, and streaming services

ADDITIONAL RESOURCES

American Collegiate Esports League (https://www.acelesports.org/): An organization that helps colleges and universities find opportunities to compete in esports conferences, leagues, and tournaments

BeRecruited (https://new.berecruited.com/): A company that helps prospective intercollegiate varsity esports student-athletes and higher education institutions connect with one another

College Esports: What You Need to Know (Shelton & Haskell, 2018): An interesting book by two faculty members in Boise State University's Educational Technology Department on how they worked with colleagues on campus to develop their institution's intercollegiate varsity esports team and an esports arena on their campus within the organizational construct of an academic department

Collegiate Starleague (https://cstarleague.com/about): A company (claiming to be the first esports collegiate gaming organization) that organizes esports competitions, including tournaments and leagues, in which individual players may sign up for teams or entire teams may sign up

Esports Integrity Coalition (https://www.esportsintegrity.com/): An organization working to prevent, detect, and address cheating in esports as well as harm to children related to esports activities

High School Esports League (https://www.highschoolesportsleague.com/): An organization supporting high schools in their efforts to host esports programs and organizing competitions for high school esports programs

Higher Education Protection Network (https://www.higheredprotection.org/): An organization promoting policies and practices in higher education intended to protect minors in their interactions with colleges and universities

Launching a College Esports Program: A Guide for Colleges and Universities (Hueber & Gehrels, 2019; available through the Association for the Promotion of Campus Activities at https://www.apca.com/): A helpful guide by two student affairs professionals on how to begin a cocurricular esports program on campus

National Association of College Admission Counseling's *Code of Ethics and Professional Practices* (https://www.nacacnet.org/globalassets/documents/advocacy-and-ethics/cepp/cepp_10_2019_final.pdf): A statement by the major higher education admissions professional association regarding ethical principles and practices in recruiting students

National Association of Collegiate Esports (https://nacesports.org/): An organization that promotes intercollegiate varsity esports through information sharing, organization of competitions, and governance

Next College Student Athlete (https://www.ncsasports.org/college-esports-scholarships/varsity-esports): A company that helps prospective intercollegiate varsity student-athletes in nearly three dozen sports, including esports, and colleges and universities connect with one another

Student League for Intercollegiate Esports (https://sliceesports.com): A company that organizes esports competitions, including tournaments and leagues, for higher education club and varsity esports teams

Tespa (https://tespa.org): An organization promoting RSO and club team esports in colleges and universities through sharing information, supporting league formation, and organizing competitions

REFERENCES

Adinoff, S., & Türkay, S. (2018). Toxic behaviors in Esports games: Player perceptions and coping strategies. *Proceedings of the 2018 Annual Symposium on Computer-Human Interaction in Play Companion Extended Abstracts.* ACM.

Alkire, A., & Franke, A. (2003, February 18). *Children on campus* [Paper presentation]. 24th Annual Conference on Law and Higher Education, Stetson University, Gulfport, Florida. https://www.stetson.edu/law/conferences/highered/archive/2003/ChildrenonCampus.pdf

Alonzo, D. (2019, February 5). The esports stars changing gaming culture from within. *Huck.* https://www.huckmag.com/p/reportage-2/esports-stars-diversity-gaming-culture/

American Association for Higher Education, American College Personnel Association, and National Association of Student Personnel Administrators. (1998). *Powerful partnerships: A shared responsibility for learning.* https://www.myacpa.org/sites/default/files/taskforce_powerful_partnerships_a_shared_responsibility_for_learning.pdf

Ashton, G. (2019, May 27). *Cheating in esports: How is it done, and how is it dealt with?* Esports Observer. https://esportsobserver.com/cheating-in-esports/

Astin, A. (1984). Student involvement: A developmental theory for higher education. *Journal of College Student Personnel, 25,* 297–308.

Banet-Weiser, S., & Miltner, K. M. (2016). #MasculinitySoFragile: Culture, structure, and networked misogyny. *Feminist Media Studies, 16*(1), 171–174.

Barr, M. J., & McClellan, G. S. (2018). *Budgets and financial management in higher education* (3rd ed.). Jossey-Bass.

Barr, M. J., McClellan, G. S., & Sandeen, A. (2014). *Making change happen in student affairs: Challenges and strategies for professionals.* Jossey-Bass.

Bauer-Wolf, J. (2019, February 12). *Video games: entertainment or sports?* Inside HigherEd. https://www.insidehighered.com/news/2019/02/12/new-frontier-college-athletics-video-games

Baugh, C. (2019). eSports go to college. *The Quad.* https://thebestschools.org/magazine/growth-college-esports/

Bell, B. C. (2019, July 26). *Gay esports caster James O'Leary sees LGBTQ support in esports blossoming.* Outsports. https://www.outsports.com/2019/7/26/8930408/gay-esports-james-oleary-lgbtq-league-legends

Ben-Porath, S. (2018, October 12). *"LOL I will never be fired": Campus free speech in the era of social media.* https://www.law.berkeley.edu/wp-content/uploads/2018/10/LOL-I-will-never-be-fired.pdf

Bet O'Clock. (n.d.). *The biggest live Esports events on the planet.* https://betoclock.com/biggest-esports-live-events/

Bloland, P. A., Stamatakos, L. C., & Rogers, R. R. (1994). *Reform in student affairs: A critique of student development.* Caps.

Bloom, B. S., Engelhart, M. D., Furst, E. J., Hill, W. H., & Krathwohl, D. R. (1956). *Taxonomy of educational objectives: The classification of educational goals. Handbook I: Cognitive domain.* David McKay.

Bolus, K. (2019, April 27). More colleges forming esports programs. *Scranton Times Tribune.* https://www.apnews.com/d50b8f38383d49788ba24fdd0fbafd06

Bowen, H. R. (1980). *Costs of higher education: How much do colleges and universities spend per student and how much should they spend?* Jossey-Bass.

Brasch, B. (2019, May 3). Fulton hospital's sports program treats video gamers like athletes. *Atlanta Journal Constitution.* https://www.ajc.com/news/local/sports-medicine-treats-video-gamers-like-athletes/Ipgwa5xDlnakY7OQaQjWwM/

Bräutigam, T. (2016, April 4). *Esports needs to face its injury problem.* Esports Observer. https://esportsobserver.com/esports-needs-face-injury-problem/

Breshnan, S. (2019, January 4). *The world's oldest esports team is gaming their way to longer lives.* CNN. https://www.cnn.com/2019/01/04/health/oldest-esports-team-gaming-longevity-intl/index.html

Brigham, R. (2019, June 7). Gay games adds esports, dodgeball. *Bay Area Reporter.* https://www.ebar.com/news/latest_news//277361

Brightman, J. (2018, June 4). *Esports deserves a "tier for elderly competitors"—Shacknews CEO.* Game Daily. https://gamedaily.biz/article/25/esports-deserves-a-tier-for-elderly-competitors-shacknews-ceo

Browning, J. (2012, December). Universities monitoring the social media accounts of their student-athletes: A recipe for disaster. *Texas Bar Journal, 75*(11), 840–843.

Buckle, C., & Mander, J. (2018). *Esports: Trends report 2018.* GlobalWebIndex. https://cdn2.hubspot.net/hubfs/304927/Downloads/Esports-report.pdf

Busta, H. (2018, October 5). *Ohio State plans esports program across 5 colleges.* Education Dive. https://www.educationdive.com/news/ohio-state-plans-esports-program-across-5-colleges/538928/

Bustamante, L. (2019, February 25). *New Jersey middle school Esports team is 1st of its kind.* NBC News Philadelphia. https://www.nbcphiladelphia.com/news/local/Middle-School-Teaches-Video-Games_Philadelphia-506314702.html

Card Player staff. (2019, April 2). *Higher level gaming to provide top-notch Esports training content for gamers.* Card Player. https://www.cardplayer.com/poker-news/23760-higher-level-gaming-to-provide-top-notch-esports-training-content-for-gamers

Carlton, C. (2017, June 19). Why "arms race" in college football is shifting from facilities to staff, leading UT's Herman to seek an "army" of analysts. *Dallas Morning News.* https://www.dallasnews.com/sports/texas-longhorns/2017/06/19/why-arms-race-in-college-football-is-shifting-from-facilities-to-staff-leading-ut-s-herman-to-seek-an-army-of-analysts/

Chambliss, D. F. (2014, September 15). The power of the personal. *Chronicle of Higher Education*. https://www.chronicle.com/article/The-Power-of-the-Personal/148743/

Chapman, G. (2018, July 11). *Disney to put live "Overwatch" eSports matches on TV*. Phys. https://phys.org/news/2018-07-disney-overwatch-esports-tv.html

Chupak, D., Weaver, S., & Meyer Bond, L. (2019). Protection of minors in higher education programs: Emerging programs, policies, and practices. *Change, 51*(2), 34–42.

Consalvo, M. (2012). *Confronting toxic gamer culture: A challenge for feminist game studies scholars*. Ada. https://adanewmedia.org/2012/11/issue1-consalvo/

D'Anastasio, C. (2019, May 23). *Shady numbers and bad business: Inside the Esports bubble*. Kotaku. https://kotaku.com/as-esports-grows-experts-fear-its-a-bubble-ready-to-po-1834982843

Data Team. (2017, October 13). Hazing deaths on American college campuses remain all too common. *The Economist*. https://www.economist.com/graphic-detail/2017/10/13/hazing-deaths-on-american-college-campuses-remain-far-too-common

Dewey, C. (2014, October 14). The only guide to Gamergate you will ever need to read. *Washington Post*. https://www.washingtonpost.com/news/the-intersect/wp/2014/10/14/the-only-guide-to-gamergate-you-will-ever-need-to-read/

DiFrancisco-Donoghue, J., Balentine, J., Schmidt, G., & Zwibel, H. (2019). Managing the health of the eSport athlete: An integrated health management model. *BMJ Open Sport & Exercise Medicine, 5*(1), e000467.

Docking, J., & Curton, C. (2015). *Crisis in higher education: A plan to save small liberal arts colleges in America*. Michigan State University Press.

Donaldson, S. (2017). I predict a riot: Making and breaking rules and norms in League of Legends. *Proceedings of DiGRA, 2017*, 11.

Doran, L. (2017, February 27). *How "eSports" is changing the college sports scene*. Inside Sources. https://www.insidesources.com/gamers-receive-college-scholarships-esports-culture-scrutiny/

Durrani, A. A. (2017, September 28). *How esports competitors prepare, mentally and physically*. Venture Beat. https://venturebeat.com/2017/09/28/how-esports-competitors-prepare-mentally-and-physically/

ESL. (2019, March 27). *ESL and Intel welcomed 174,000 fans at the world's most attended esports event*. https://about.eslgaming.com/blog/2019/03/esl-and-intel-welcomed-174000-fans-at-worlds-most-attended-esports-event-and-most-watched-esl-csgo-tournament-ever/

Egency. (2018, April 13). *The lucrative Esports business is attracting big-name sponsors*. https://www.egencyglobal.com/2018/04/13/the-lucrative-esports-business-is-attracting-big-name-sponsors/

Electronic Entertainment Design and Research. (2015). *Esports consumer analysis whitepaper*. http://progamedev.net/wp-content/uploads/2015/11/EEDAR_%E2%80%93_eSports_Consumer_Analysis_2015.pdf

Entertainment Software Association. (2019). *2019 essential facts about the computer and video game industry.* http://www.theesa.com/about-esa/industry-facts/

Esports Integrity Coalition. (2016). *Threats to the integrity of esports: A risk analysis.* Author.

Esports Integrity Coalition. (2019a). *Child protection.* https://www.esportsintegrity.com/home/child-protection/

Esports Integrity Coalition. (2019b). *What we do.* https://www.esportsintegrity.com/about-us/what-we-do/

Fischer, B. (2018, January 9). Sources: Overwatch League-Twitch deal worth at least $90M. *Sports Business Daily.* https://www.sportsbusinessdaily.com/Daily/Closing-Bell/2018/01/09/overwatch.aspx

Funk, D. C., Pizzo, A. D., & Baker, B. J. (2018). Esport management: Embracing eSport education and research opportunities. *Sport Management Review, 21*, 7–13.

Gabler, N. (2019, August 2). Ole Miss researching health implications of esports. *Oxford Eagle.* https://oxfordeagle.com/2019/08/02/ole-miss-researching-health-implications-of-esports/

Gallucio, B. (2019, April 12). *Five eSports podcasts that will help up your game.* I Heart Radio. https://www.iheart.com/content/2019-04-12-five-esports-podcasts-that-will-help-you-up-your-game/

Gambling Sites. (n.d.). *Most popular Esports games as of 2019.* https://www.gamblingsites.com/esports-betting/games/#multiplayer_games

Gamer Sensei. (2019). *Take your game to the next level.* https://www.gamersensei.com/

Gladwell, M. (2000). *The tipping point: How little things can make a big difference.* Little, Brown.

Goldman Sachs. (2019). *eSports joins the big leagues.* https://www.goldmansachs.com/insights/pages/infographics/e-sports/index.html

Gough, C. (2017, October 11). *Number of players of selected eSprots gamers worldwide as of August 2017 (in million).* Statista. https://www.statista.com/statistics/506923/esports-games-number-players-global/

Gough, C. (2019, May 22). *Number of unique viewers of selected eSports tournaments worldwide as of January 2018.* Statista. https://www.statista.com/statistics/507491/esports-tournaments-by-number-viewers-global/

Gunn, O. (2019, May 9). The rise of eSports in the queer community. *The Georgia Voice.* https://thegavoice.com/community/the-rise-of-esports-in-the-queer-community/

Haenfler, R. (2004). Rethinking subcultural resistance. *Journal of Contemporary Ethnography, 33*(4), 406–436.

Hallmann, K., & Giel, T. (2018). eSports—Competitive sports or recreational activity? *Sports Management Review, 21*, 14–20.

Hamari, J., & Sjöblom, M. (2017). What is eSports and why do people watch it? *Internet Research, 27*, 211–232.

Harvey. (2017). *eSports in middle school athletics.* Donors Choose. https://www.donorschoose.org/project/esports-in-middle-school-athletics/2695315/

Havighurst, R. J. (1952). *Human development and education.* Longmans, Green.

Hayward, A. (2019, April 12). *Cars, drinks, and clothes: non-endemic sponsor recap for Q1 2019*. Esports Observer. https://esportsobserver.com/non-endemic-sponsors-q12019/

Heilweil, R. (2019, January 21). *Infoporn: College Esports players are cashing in big*. Wired. https://www.wired.com/story/infoporn-college-esports-players-cashing-in-big/

Heitner, D. (2016, November 17). Multi-million dollar big data deal paves the way for esports betting. *Forbes*. https://www.forbes.com/sites/darrenheitner/2016/11/17/multi-million-dollar-big-data-deal-paves-the-way-for-esports-betting/

Hennen, A. (2019, March 1). *Collegiate Esports programs are here to stay*. James G. Allen Center for Academic Renewal. https://www.jamesgmartin.center/2019/03/collegiate-esports-programs-are-here-to-stay/

Hennick, C. (2019, January 11). Esports programs start to pop up in K-12 schools. *Ed Tech*. https://edtechmagazine.com/k12/article/2019/01/esports-programs-start-pop-k-12-schools

High School Esports League. (2019). *High School Esports League*. https://www.highschoolesportsleague.com/

Holmes, J. (2019, March 7). At the NBA 2K League draft, I witnessed the surreal future of what it means to go pro. *Esquire*. https://www.esquire.com/sports/a26684917/nba-2k-league-draft-esports/

Hueber, C. M., & Gehrels, D. (2019). *Launching a college esports program: A guide for colleges and universities*: Association for the Promotion of Campus Activities.

Ingraham, C. (2018, August 27). The massive popularity of esports, in charts. *Washington Post*. https://www.washingtonpost.com/business/2018/08/27/massive-popularity-esports-charts/

Jacobs, H. (2015, May 11). Here's the insane training schedule of a 20-something professional gamer. *Business Insider*. https://www.businessinsider.com/pro-gamers-explain-the-insane-training-regimen-they-use-to-stay-on-top-2015-5

Jackson, V. (2016). *Diversity & inclusion in collegiate Esports: Challenges, opportunities, and interventions*. AnyKey. http://www.anykey.org/wp-content/uploads/Diversity-and-Inclusion-in-Collegiate-Esports.pdf

Kaplin, W. A., & Lee, B. A. (2013). *The law of higher education* (5th ed.). Jossey-Bass.

Kaplin, W. A., Lee, B. A., Hutchens, N. H., & Rooksby, J. H. (2019). *The law of higher education* (6th ed.). Jossey-Bass.

Keeler, S. (2018, November 26). *Growth of esports offers smaller colleges chance to compete with big boys*: Global Sports Matters. https://globalsportmatters.com/youth/2018/11/26/growth-esports-offering-smaller-colleges-chance-compete/

Kids in the Game. (2019, January 30). *Kids in the game (KING) announces launch of first-ever NYC middle school Esports league*. PR Newswire. https://www.prnewswire.com/news-releases/kids-in-the-game-king-announces-launch-of-first-ever-nyc-middle-school-esports-league-300787216.html

Kozinets, R. V. (1999). E-tribalized marketing? The strategic implications of virtual communities of consumption. *European Management Journal, 17*(3), 252–264.

Kuh, G. D. (1996). Guiding principles for creating seamless learning environments for undergraduates. *Journal of College Student Development*, *37*(2), 135–148.

Lajka, A. (2018, December 21). *Esports players burn out young as the grind takes mental, physical toll*. CBS News. https://www.cbsnews.com/news/esports-burnout-in-video-gaming-cbsn-originals/

Lake, P. (2011). *Foundations of higher education law and policy: Basic legal rules, concepts, and principles for student affairs*. NASPA.

Legal Sports Report. (2018). *Legal esports betting: Overview of the esports gambling vertical*. https://www.legalsportsreport.com/esports-betting/

Liao, S. (2019, August 1). *She's 13 and was born deaf. Now Ewok is making history playing "Fortnite"*. CNN. https://www.cnn.com/2019/08/01/tech/ewok-fortnite-soleil-wheeler/index.html

Lingler, S. (2016, March 6). The complicated past (and future) of esports on TV. *The Kernel*. https://kernelmag.dailydot.com/issue-sections/headline-story/16083/eleague-esports-tv-history/

List of highest-grossing video game franchises. (2019, July 24). Wikipedia. https://en.wikipedia.org/w/index.php?title=List_of_highest-grossing_video_game_franchises&oldid=907710734

Liu, K. (2019, June 27). *Top 10 university eSports programs & facilities in the US*. Lineups Betting. https://www.lineups.com/betting/top-10-university-esports-facilities-and-programs-in-the-us/

Lucich, R., & Gehrels, D. (2019). *Esports player's handbook*. Schreiner University.

Lumb, D. (2018, August 3). *College Esports is uncharted territory, so smaller schools are staking their claim*. Kotaku. https://kotaku.com/collegiate-esports-is-uncharted-territory-so-smaller-s-1828070908

Macey, J., & Humari, J. (2018). Investigating relationships between video gaming, spectating esports, and gambling. *Computers in Human Behavior*, *80*, 344–353.

Mayhew, M. J., Rockenbach, A. N., Bowman, N. A., Seifert, T. A., & Wolniak, G. C. (2016). *How college affects students: 21st century evidence that higher education works* (3rd ed.). Jossey-Bass.

McClellan, G. S. (2019, Fall). Fifth wave rising: Esports, fantasy sports, & the expansion of legalized gambling. *Leadership Exchange*, *17*(3), 24–29.

McClellan, G. S., & Arnett, R. S. (2019, February 3). *ESports: Emerging law & policy issues* [PowerPoint presentation]. Stetson University National Conference on Law in Higher Education, Clearwater, FL.

McClellan, G. S., Hardy, T. W., & Caswell, J. (Eds.). (2006). *Getting ahead of the game: Understanding and addressing gambling on campus*. (New Directions for Student Services, No. 113). Jossey-Bass.

McClellan, G. S., & Hutchens, N. H. (In press). *Shared Governance, Law, and Policy in Student Affairs Practice*. Thompson.

McClellan, G. S., & Winters, K. C. (2006). Gambling: An old school new wave challenge for higher education in the twenty-first century. In G. S. McClellan, T. W. Hardy, and J. Caswell (Eds.), *Gambling on campus* (New Directions for Student Services, No. 113, pp. 9–23). Jossey-Bass.

McLuhan, M. (1970). *Culture is our business*. McGraw-Hill.
McNair, K. (2019, June 5). *No end in site in athletics facilities arms race*. CBS Sports. https://www.cbssports.com/college-football/news/no-end-in-sight-in-athletics-facilities-arms-race/
Meola, A. (2018, January 12). *The biggest companies sponsoring Esports tournaments*. Business Insider. https://www.businessinsider.com/top-esports-sponsors-gaming-sponsorships-2018-1
Mills, D. B. (2003). Assembling the project team. In J. M. Price (Ed.), *Planning and achieving successful student affairs facilities projects* (New Directions for Student Services, No. 101, pp. 29–38). Jossey-Bass.
Mintz, S. (2019, April). *Are today's college students more psychologically fragile than in the past?* Inside HigherEd. https://www.insidehighered.com/blogs/higher-ed-gamma/are-today's-college-students-more-psychologically-fragile-past
Moore, K. (2017, February 21). *The rise in college Esports scholarships*. Esports Observer. https://esportsobserver.com/esports-scholarships/
Moss, R. (2017, September 15). *Build, gather, brawl, repeat: The history of real-time strategy games*. Ars Technica. https://arstechnica.com/gaming/2017/09/build-gather-brawl-repeat-the-history-of-real-time-strategy-games/
Mulkerin, T. (2016, May 13). *eSports has a racism problem*. Business Insider. https://www.businessinsider.com/the-esports-racism-problem-2016-5
Murray, T. (2018, June 1). *Overwatch League Finals sell out in two weeks*. Esports Observer. https://esportsobserver.com/overwatch-league-finals-sold-out/
Myers, M. (2018, July 11). *Esports player's use of homophobic slur sets off unexpectedly long debate*. Kokatu. https://kotaku.com/esports-players-use-of-homophobic-slur-sets-off-unexpec-1827514527
National Association of College Admission Counseling. (2018). *NACAC's Code of Ethics and Professional Practices*. https://www.nacacnet.org/globalassets/documents/advocacy-and-ethics/cepp/cepp_10_2019_final.pdf
National Association of Collegiate Esports. (2019a). *About*. https://nacesports.org/about/
National Association of Collegiate Esports. (2019b). *Esports*. https://nacesports.org/what-is-e-sports/games/
National Association of Collegiate Esports. (2019c). *Convention recap*. https://nacesports.org/wp-content/uploads/2019/07/2019-Convention-Recap.pdf
National Federation of State High School Associations. (2019). *Esports*. https://www.nfhs.org/sports-resource-content/esports/
Newcomb, A. (2019). January 31). *The world's first-ever middle school E-sports league mixes physical and virtual play*. Fortune. https://fortune.com/2019/01/31/middle-school-e-sports-league/
Newzoo. (2019). *Most watched games on Twitch & YouTube*. https://newzoo.com/insights/rankings/top-games-twitch-youtube/
Next College Student Athlete. (2019). *List of colleges with varsity esports programs*. https://www.ncsasports.org/college-esports-scholarships/varsity-esports

Nguyen, T. (2019). In growing "wild west" of Esports, programs rush to recruit best players. *The Chronicle of Higher Education.* https://www.chronicle.com/article/In-Growing-Wild-West-of/245560

North American Scholastic Esports Federation. (2019). *North American Scholastic Esports Federation.* https://www.esportsfed.org/

Partners in Leadership. (n.d.). 31 quotes from great leaders to make employees happier at work. *Inc.* https://www.inc.com/partners-in-leadership/31-quotes-from-great-leaders-to-improve-workplace-satisfaction-for-employees.html

Pei, A. (2019, April 4). *This esports giant draws more viewers than the Super Bowl, and it's expected to get even bigger.* CNBC. https://www.cnbc.com/2019/04/14/league-of-legends-gets-more-viewers-than-super-bowlwhats-coming-next.html

PEN America. (2017, June 15). *And campus for all: Diversity, inclusion, and freedom of speech at U.S. universities.* https://pen.org/wp-content/uploads/2017/06/PEN_campus_report_06.15.2017.pdf

Peterson, L. (2018, March 27). *Why aren't more black kids going into pro esports?* The Undefeated. https://theundefeated.com/features/why-arent-more-black-kids-going-pro-in-esports/

Pine, B. J., & Gilmore, J. H. (1998). Welcome to the experience economy. *Harvard Business Review, 76*(4), 97–105.

Quintana, C. (2019, July 30). Another college admissions scandal? To get financial aid, parents lose custody of their children. *USA Today.* https://www.usatoday.com/story/news/education/2019/07/30/college-financial-aid-custody-transfer-guardianship-loophole-admissions-scandal/1868220001/

Quote Investigator. (2013, October 20). *It's difficult to make predictions, especially about the future.* https://quoteinvestigator.com/2013/10/20/no-predict/

Rapoza, K. (2019, May 29). Global Esports popularity give gamer companies reason to be bullish. *Forbes.* https://www.forbes.com/sites/kenrapoza/2019/05/29/global-esports-popularity-give-gamer-companies-reason-to-be-bullish/

Reames, M. (2018, June 21). *The overlap between STEM education and Esports.* Sports Techie. https://www.sporttechie.com/stem-esports-league-of-legends-columbia-college-oregon-syracuse/

Redd, D. (2018, July). College athletics arms race shows no signs of slowing. *Charleston Gazette Mail.* https://www.athleticbusiness.com/college/college-athletics-arms-race-shows-no-signs-of-slowing.html

Reimer, J. (2005, October 10). *The evolution of gaming: Computers, consoles, and arcades.* Ars Technica. https://arstechnica.com/features/2005/10/gaming-evolution/2/

Rodgers, B. (1977). *Rationalizing sports policies: Sport in social context: International comparisons.* Council of Europe.

Rose, I. N. (1980). The legalization and control of casino gambling. *Fordham Urban Law Journal, 8,* 245.

Rovell, D. (2017, January 19). *The Big Ten Network and Riot Games launch the BTN League of Legends season.* ESPN. https://www.espn.com/esports/story/_/id/18508637/the-big-ten-network-riot-games-partner-league-legends-college-esports

Ruvalcaba, O., Shulze, J., Kim, A., Berzenski, S. R., & Otten, M. P. (2018). Women's experiences in eSports: Gendered differences in peer and spectator feedback during competitive video game play. *Journal of Sports and Social Issues, 42*(4), 295–311.

Seemiller, C., & Grace, M. (2015). *Generation Z goes to college.* Jossey-Bass.

Selingo, J. J. (2018). *The new generation of students: How colleges can recruit, teach, and serve Gen Z.* The Chronicle of Higher Education.

Seo, Y. (2013). Electronic sports: A new marketing landscape of the experience economy. *Journal of Marketing Management, 29*(13–14), 1542–1560.

Shelton, B. E., & Haskell, C. (2018). *College esports: What you need to know.* Baxajaunak Technology.

Smith, N. (2018, May 10). Esports training facility brings gaming another step closer to traditional pro sports. *Washington Post.* https://www.washingtonpost.com/sports/esports-training-facility-brings-gaming-another-step-closer-to-traditional-pro-sports/2018/05/10/c102e684-4e2f-11e8-84a0-458a1aa9ac0a_story.html

Snyder, E. M., Huchens, N. H., Jones, W. A., & Sun, J. C. (2015). Social media policies in intercollegiate athletics: The speech and privacy rights of student-athletes. *Journal for the Study of Sports and Athletics in Education, 9*(1), 50–74.

Statista. (2015, September 9). *eSports betting market revenue worldwide in 2015 and 2020.* https://www.statista.com/statistics/618985/espots-betting-market-revenue-worldwide/

Stoller, E. (2019, May 16). *An epic update on collegiate Esports.* Inside Higher Ed. https://www.insidehighered.com/blogs/student-affairs-and-technology/epic-update-collegiate-esports

Strickland, W. (2019, March 1). *MLB likely to enter esports in 2019.* DOT Esports. https://dotesports.com/business/news/mlb-likely-to-enter-esports-in-2019

Sun, J. C., & McClellan, G. S. (2019). *Student clashes on campus: A leadership guide to free speech.* Routledge.

Swerdlow, A. (2019, February 4). *NASCAR is racing into esports. Here's how it can succeed.* Venture Beat. https://venturebeat.com/2019/02/04/nascar-is-racing-into-esports-heres-how-it-can-succeed/

Tespa. (2019). *So tell me . . . What is Tespa?* https://tespa.org/about

Tespa. (2019, July 21). Wikipedia. Retrieved July 31, 2019. https://en.wikipedia.org/wiki/Tespa

Thamel, P. (2012, March 30). Tracking Twitter, raising red flags. *New York Times.* https://www.nytimes.com/2012/03/31/sports/universities-track-athletes-online-raising-legal-concerns.html

Tiedemann, C. (2004, September 24). *Sport (and culture of physical motion) for historians, an approach to make the central term(s) more precise* [Paper presentation].

IX International CESH-Congress, Crotone, Italy. www.http://kulturwiss.info/tiedemann/documents/VortragCrotone2004Englisch.pdf.

Tran, C. (2019, April 8). *How to design an Esports arena*. City Lab. https://www.citylab.com/design/2019/04/esports-video-games-philadelphia-fusion-arena-tech-design/586126/

Tsitsos, W., & Nixon, H. L. II. (2012). The star wars arms race in college athletics. *Journal of Sports & Social Issues, 36*(1), 68–88.

University of California, Irvine. (2016, March 30). *UCI to launch first-of-its-kind official esports initiative in the fall.* https://news.uci.edu/2016/03/30/uci-to-launch-first-of-its-kind-official-e-sports-initiative-in-the-fall/

University of California, Irvine Esports. (n.d.). *Reporting.* https://esports.uci.edu/reporting/

University of California, Irvine Esports. (2017). *2017-2018 Inclusivity Plan.* https://esports.uci.edu/wp-content/uploads/sites/3/2017/09/Inclusivity-Plan.pdf

University of Utah. (2017, April 5). *Varsity Esports comes to the U.* https://unews.utah.edu/varsity-esports-comes-to-the-u/

Van Allen, E. (2019, January 26). *How a trash-talking furry became Esports' dominant player.* Wired. https://www.wired.com/story/all-hail-the-fox/

Wagner, M. G. (n.d.). *On the scientific relevance of eSports.* https://www.wired.com/story/all-hail-the-fox/.https://www.researchgate.net/profile/Michael_Wagner12/publication/220968200_On_the_Scientific_Relevance_of_eSports/links/00b4952589870231be000000.pdf

Weller, C. (2016, April 4). *A new eSports scholarship will award $20,000 to student gamers.* Business Insider. https://www.businessinsider.com/new-esports-scholarship-for-student-gamers-2016-3

Wolf, J. (2017, February 17). *The NBA and esports: How we got here.* ESPN. https://www.espn.com/esports/story/_/id/18702213/the-nba-esports-how-got-here

Yan, H. (2019, March 19). *What we know so far in the college admissions cheating scandal.* CNN. https://www.cnn.com/2019/03/13/us/what-we-know-college-admissions-cheating-scandal/index.html

Zavaleta, L. (2018, January 4). Dallas gamer suspended for telling gay Houston player to "suck a fat c-ck. *Out Smart.* http://www.outsmartmagazine.com/2018/01/dallas-gamer-suspended-for-telling-gay-houston-player-to-suck-a-fat-c-ck/

Zimmerman, E. (2018, November 6). Universities invest in Esports academic opportunities. *Ed Tech.* https://edtechmagazine.com/higher/article/2018/11/universities-invest-esports-academic-opportunities

Administrative Action, Legislation, and Legal Cases

Chaplinsky v. New Hampshire, 315 U.S. 568, (1942).
Child Online Protection Act (47 U.S.C. § 231).
Child Pornography Prevention Act of 1996 (18 U.S.C. §§ 2251 et seq.).

Central Hudson Gas & Electric Cor. v Public Service Commission of New York, 447 U.S. 557 (1980).
Cohen v. Brown, 991 F.2d 888 (1st Cir. 1993).
Davis v. Monroe County Board of Education, 526 U.S. 629 (1999)
Jacobellis v. Ohio, 378 U.S. 184 (1964).
Miller v. California, 413 U.S. 15 (1973).
Planned Parenthood of Columbia/Willamette, Inc., et al. v. American Coalition of Life Advocates, et al., 290 F.3d 1058 (9th Cir. 2002).
Title IX of the Educational Amendments Act of 1972, Public Law No. 92-318, 86 Stat. 235, codified at 20 U.S.C. §§ 1681–1688.
Title V of the Telecommunications Act of 1996 (110 Stat. 56).
United States v. Alkhabaz aka Jake Baker, 104 F.3d 1492 (6th Cir. 1997).
Virginia v. Black, 538 U.S. 343 (2003).

ABOUT THE AUTHORS

George S. McClellan is associate professor of higher education at the University of Mississippi. Prior to joining the students and colleagues there, he served students for 35 years in a variety of student affairs professional positions, including service as senior student affairs officer at both Indiana University–Purdue University Fort Wayne (IPFW) and Dickinson State University.

He is the (co)author or (co)editor of numerous books, chapters, and articles on student affairs and higher education. His books and monographs include *Shared Governance, Law, and Policy in Student Affairs Professional Practice* with N. Hutchens (forthcoming, Thompson), *Student Clashes on Campus: A Leadership Guide to Free Speech* with J. Sun (2019, Routledge), *A Good Job: Campus Employment as a High-Impact Practice* with K. Creager and M. Savoca (2018, Stylus Publishing), *Budgets and Financial Management in Higher Education* with M. Barr (2011 & 2018, Jossey-Bass), *The Handbook for Student Affairs Administration* with J. Stringer (2009 & 2016, Jossey-Bass), *Making Change Happen in Student Affairs: Challenges and Strategies* with M. Barr and A. Sandeen (2014, Jossey-Bass), *The Handbook for College Athletics and Recreation Administration* with C. King and D. Rockey Jr. (2012, Jossey-Bass), *Stepping Up and Stepping Out: Helping Students Transition to the Real World* with J. Parker (2012, Jossey-Bass), *In Search of Safer Communities: Emerging Practices for Student Affairs in Addressing Campus Violence* with M. Jablonski, E. Zdziarksi, D. Ambler, R. Barnett-Terry, L. Cook, J. Dunkle, R. Gatti, E. Griego, and J. Kindle (New Directions for Student Services, 2008, Jossey-Bass), *Gambling on Campus* with T. Hardy and J. Caswell (New Directions for Student Services, 2006, Jossey-Bass), and *Serving Native American Students* with M. Fox and S. Lowe (New Directions for Student Services, 2005, Jossey-Bass).

McClellan received the Outstanding Contribution to Research in American Indian Higher Education Award from the Native American Network of the American College Personnel Association in 2002 and the Annuit Coeptis Senior Scholar Award from that association in 2017. He was recognized with the George D. Kuh Award for Outstanding Contribution to Literature and/or Research in 2020 from NASPA and by the NASPA Foundation as a Pillar of the Profession in 2010. He received his PhD in higher education from the University of Arizona (2003). Both his MSEd in higher education (1998) and BA in English and American literature (1982) were earned from Northwestern University.

Ryan S. Arnett has been involved with esports for the last 5 years and counting. Arnett has been a competitive player, analyst, recruiter, coach, and team owner in the world of esports, most notably as the current owner of HammerHead Gaming, an organization that competes, provides entertainment, and offers agency services to players in the industry. Arnett recently earned his JD from the Stetson University College of Law and holds a BA in political science and Spanish from Florida Southern College.

Charles M. Hueber is the dean of students at Schreiner University. Hueber has worked in higher education for over 20 years. He has served as a speaker and consultant to a variety of universities and businesses in leadership development, customer service, and social integration. Hueber is a self-proclaimed nerd and has a passion for esports and gaming and has spent the past few years conducting his scholarly research on the impact of esports on universities and colleges. Hueber earned his EdD from Texas A&M University at Commerce in higher educational administration and holds BA and MA degrees in counseling and psychology, both from Stephen F. Austin State University.

INDEX

ACEL. *See* American Collegiate Esports League
advisers
   finding the right, 39–40
   staff leaders as, 53
Aimbot, 127
Alkire, A., 104
amateurism, 123–24
American Collegiate Esports League (ACEL), 36, 127
Andre, Thomas, 108
arms race, 119–20
attendance data, 9, 10

Banet-Weiser, S., 89
Barr, M. J., 47–48, 54–55, 115
behavior
   expectations, 57–58
   toxic, 78, 84–85, 86–90, 93–96
Ben-Porath, S., 102
Bloom, B. S., 44
boundary setting, 76–77
Bowen, H. R., 120
business, 18–20

caster
   becoming a, 74
   definition of, 127
   Shoutcaster, 129
CDA. *See* Communications Decency Act
Central Hudson Gas & Electric Corp. v. Public Service Commission of New York, 99
channels
   communication, 60–61
   definition of, 127
Chaplinsky v. New Hampshire, 97
cheating, 117–18
childhood experiences, 73
child protection, 104–6, 116
club teams
   cocurriculum, 24
   definition of, 127
   at SU, 59–61, 66–71
   varsity teams compared to, 43–44
coaches
   employment of, 55–56
   finding the right, 39–40
   game selection by, 58
   mentoring by, 53
   player expectations set by, 57–58
   roster and schedules set by, 58–59
   salaries, 35
   sample description on role of, 41–42
   staff leaders as, 52–53
COC. *See* College Operating Cost
cocurriculum and curriculum, 22–25
code of conduct, 95–96
Cohen v. Brown, 91
College Operating Cost (COC), 37, 38
colleges and universities
   curriculum and cocurriculum elements of, 22–25
   guidance and governance for, 26–27
   motivations behind participation of, 21–22
   organizational structure within, 25–26
   strategies for, 113–15
   student-athlete recommendations for, 80–85

Collegiate Starleague (CSL), 36, 61, 62, 127
commercial speech, 99
communication channels, 60–61
Communications Decency Act (CDA), 105
competition climate. *See also* toxic behavior
   as challenge, 116
   as opportunity, 121–22
competition schedule/structure
   as challenge, 115
   creation of, 36, 61–62
   as opportunity, 120–21
   sample of esports arena, 63–64
consoles
   definition of, 127
   gaming computer over, 74
   PC-based games compared to, 93
costs/expenses
   first-year operating, 34–35
   fundraising for, 35, 40
   as obstacle, 33–34
   for outfitting arena space, 49
   ROI in relation to, 36–38
   start-up, 34
   student-athletes on, 77
counselors, 53
Crisis in Higher Education (Docking), 28
CSL. *See* Collegiate Starleague
Culture Is Our Business (McLuhan), 1
curriculum and cocurriculum, 22–25

data
   attendance, 9, 10
   lack of reliable, 119
   player participation, 8–9
   reliable, 122
   viewership, 13–14, 15, 16
Davis v. Monroe County Board of Education, 92–93
defamation, 98
deviant play, 87, 127

DiFrancisco-Donoghue, J., 107–9, 110
digital speech, 102–3
Discord, 60–61
Discounts/Scholarships (D/S), 37, 38
Docking, Jeffery, 28
Donaldson, S., 87
doping, 117, 127
D/S. *See* Discounts/Scholarships

educators, 53–55
Electronic Entertainment Design and Research (EEDAR), 8–9, 14
ENE. *See* Expected New Enrollment
equipment expenses, 34
ESIC. *See* Esports Integrity Coalition
esports. *See also specific topics*
   arms race, 119–20
   attendance data, 9, 10
   as business, 18–20
   connection between higher education and, 20–27
   defining, 2, 3, 127
   as experience economy, 7
   learning about, 9–13
   opportunities from, 1
   player participation data, 8–9
   traditional sport compared to, 3, 14–18
   types of, 4–6
   viewership data, 13–14, 15, 16
esports arenas
   comfortability of space in, 49
   definition of, 127
   developing space for, 49
   Fusion Arena, 9
   identifying space for, 48–49
   management of, 62–64
   outfitting space for, 49
   planning dilemma and strategies for, 47–48
Esports Integrity Coalition (ESIC)
   on cheating, 117, 118
   on child protection, 104, 116

definition of, 128
esports programs
  case study on creating structure within, 56–61
  challenges ahead for, 115–20
  curriculum and cocurriculum elements of, 22–25
  feasibility study for, 31–38
  foundational steps for, 29–31
  hope for, 124–25
  identifying key individuals for, 38–42
  inclusive model of, 42–43, 95–96
  learning outcomes for, 44–46
  management of, 51–65
  motivations for developing, 21–22
  opportunities ahead for, 120–24
  strategies for establishing, 113–15
  student-athlete recommendations for, 80–85
ethnicity of fans, 94
exempted speech, 97–99
Expected New Enrollment (ENE), 37, 38
expenses. *See* costs/expenses
experience economy
  definition of, 128
  esports as, 7
external speech, 100–101

faculty, 40
fans, 94
feasibility study, 31–38
fighting games, 5, 87, 128
fighting words, 97
First Amendment, 96–97
first-person shooter games (FPS), 4–5, 128
first-year operating costs, 34–35
flaming, 128
foundational steps, 29–31
FPS. *See* first-person shooter games
Franke, A., 104
freemium model, 128

free speech, 96–103
friendships, 75–76
fundraising, 35, 40
Funk, D. C., 2, 17, 87
Fusion Arena, 9

gambling
  as challenge, 118–19
  fifth wave of, 106
  legality of, 107
Gamergate, 89
Gamer's Guild
  creed, 66–71
  structure, 59–61
gaming computers
  over console, 74
  definition of, 128
  PC, 93
gaymer, 88, 128
Giel, T., 15–17
Gilmore, J. H., 7
Gladwell, Malcolm, 38
GLHF!. *See* "Good luck, and have fun!"
goals, 32
"Good luck, and have fun!" (GLHF!), 125, 128
governance
  concerns about, 109–12
  guidance and, 26–27
  as opportunity, 120–21
  by student-athletes, 60, 66–71

Hallmann, K., 15–17
Hamari, J., 3
harassment
  deviant play as, 87, 127
  legal definition of, 98–99
  online, 86
  Title IX and, 90–93
hazing, 85
health
  concerns about, 107–9
  medical support model for, 110

recommendations on mental and
physical, 80–82
self-care for, 78
higher education. *See also* colleges and universities
connection between esports and, 20–27
free speech rights in, 96–103
survival of, 28–29
toxic behavior addressed by, 93–96
High School Esports League, 11
homophobia, 86–88
Hopper, Chris, 21

Imagineering, 47
Inclusion in Esports Task Force, 96
inclusive model
code of conduct for, 95–96
creation of, 42–43
information gathering, 32
injuries, 107–9, 110
Intent to Compete form, 111
intercollegiate varsity sports
cocurriculum, 24–25
definition of, 128
governance concerns with, 109–12
Intergalactic Spacewar Olympics, 20–21
internal speech, 100–101
intimidation and threats, 97–98

K-16 education, 11–12
Kaplin, W. A., 102–3, 104
Kozinets, R. V., 1

LANs. *See* local area networks
law
child protection, 105
of the few, 38
free speech, 96–103
gambling, 107
Title IX, 90–93
law school experiences, 74–79

LCS. *See* League of Legends Championship Series
League of Legends (LoL)
definition of, 128
future aspirations for, 21
homophobia issue in, 88
introduction to, 73
practices, 59
League of Legends Championship Series (LCS)
definition of, 128
viewers of, 13
learning
about esports, 9–13
outcomes, 44–46
principles, 54–55
LGBTQ members, 88, 128
life lessons, 75–76
lifelong learning, 12
local area networks (LANs), 2, 128
LoL. *See* League of Legends

Major League Baseball, 20
Major League Soccer (MLS), 20
manipulation. *See* tournament structure manipulation
match-fixing, 117, 118, 128
McLean, Dominique, 87–88
McLuhan, Marshal, 1
media
revenue from, 19
social, 103
membership fees, 34–35
Miller, Terrence, 93
Miller v. California, 98
Miltner, K. M., 89
minors. *See* child protection
Mintz, Steven, 53
misogyny, 86–87, 88–90
MLS. *See* Major League Soccer
MOBA. *See* multiplayer online battle arena games
Moss, R., 5–6

motivations, 21–22
multiplayer online battle arena games (MOBA), 4, 129

NACE. *See* National Association of Collegiate Esports
NAIA. *See* National Association of Intercollegiate Athletics
NASCAR, 20
NASEF. *See* North American Scholastic Esports Federation
National Association of Collegiate Esports (NACE)
  alternative to, 121
  on amateurism, 124
  definition of, 129
  governance by, 26–27, 111–12
  NCAA and, 24
  on prize money, 82
National Association of Intercollegiate Athletics (NAIA), 24, 27, 118, 121
National Basketball Association (NBA), 20
National Collegiate Athletic Association (NCAA)
  on esports, 24–25
  on gambling, 107, 118
National Collegiate eSports Association (NCeSPA), 129
National Federation of State High School Associations (NFHS), 11, 36
National Football League (NFL), 20
National Hockey League (NHL), 20
National Junior College Athletic Association (NJCAA), 24, 27, 118, 121
NBA. *See* National Basketball Association
NCAA. *See* National Collegiate Athletic Association
NCeSPA. *See* National Collegiate esports Association

networked misogyny, 89
NFHS. *See* National Federation of State High School Associations
NFL. *See* National Football League
NHL. *See* National Hockey League
Nintendo 64, 73, 129
NJCAA. *See* National Junior College Athletic Association
North American Scholastic Esports Federation (NASEF), 11

obscenity, 98
O'Leary, James, 88
online harassment, 86
online learning, 10–11
organizational structure, 25–26
Overwatch
  definition of, 129
  practices, 59
  release of, 73–74
Overwatch League
  homophobia issue in, 88
  Twitch deal with, 19
Overwatch University League
  caster of, 74
  definition of, 129

partnership opportunities, 123
PC-based games, 93
Peterson, L., 93, 94
Pine, B. J., 7
Planned Parenthood of Columbia/Willamette, Inc. v. American Coalition of Life Advocates, 98
players. *See also* student-athletes; *specific players*
  behavior expectations of, 57–58
  participation data on, 8–9
  roster selection, 58–59
PlayVS, 11, 21
POC. *See* Program Operating Cost
Powerful Partnerships (Barr), 54–55
priming, 95, 129
prize money, 77, 82–83

professional sports, 19–20
Program Operating Cost (POC), 37, 38

racing. *See* sports and racing
racism, 86–87, 93
real-time strategy games (RTS), 5–6, 129
recognized/registered student organization (RSO)
   cocurriculum, 24
   definition of, 129
recruitment
   expenses, 35
   of key individuals, 38–42
   of students, 35–36, 122–23
return on investment (ROI), 36–38
revenue sources, 18–20
Rodgers, B., 15–16
ROI. *See* return on investment
RSO. *See* recognized/registered student organization
RTS. *See* real-time strategy games
Ruvalcaba, O., 90

safety/security, 49, 62–63
salaries, 35
Schreiner University (SU)
   esports program structures at, 56–61
   Gamer's Guild creed, 66–71
security. *See* safety/security
self-care, 78
Seo, Y., 3, 7
Shack Champions League, 12
Shoutcaster, 129
Silver Snipers, 12
Sjöblom, M., 3
SLICE. *See* Student League for Intercollegiate Esports
socialization, 78–79, 83–85
social media content, 103
Space Invaders competition, 8
speech

commercial, 99
digital, 102–3
exempted, 97–99
First Amendment on, 96–97
internal and external, 100–101
space for, 101
student-athlete, 103
sponsorship, 19–20
sports
   criteria for, 15–16
   defining, 2
   esports compared to traditional, 3, 14–18
   professional, 19–20
sports and racing games, 6, 20, 129
spot-fixing, 117, 118, 129
staff leaders
   as advisers, 53
   as coaches, 52–53
   as counselors, 53
   as educators, 53–55
start-up costs, 34
stereotypes, 79
streaming
   definition of, 129
   on Twitch, 13–14, 15, 19, 130
   on YouTube, 13–14, 16
student-athletes
   on boundary setting, 76–77
   on childhood, 73
   on costs, 77
   expectations of, 57–58
   on friendships and life lessons, 75–76
   game selection by, 60
   governance by, 60, 66–71
   Intent to Compete form for, 111
   mentoring of, 53
   on prize money, 77, 82–83
   recommendations for, 80–85
   roster and schedules of, 58–59
   on self-care, 78
   on socialization, 78–79, 83–85
   social media content of, 103

on stereotypes, 79
story of personal experiences as, 72–80
on toxic behavior, 78
on turning pro while in law school, 74–79
on undergraduate years, 73–74
Student League for Intercollegiate Esports (SLICE), 36, 61, 62, 129
students
　level of involvement of current, 33
　ownership by, 39
　qualities of current generation of, 52
　recruitment of, 35–36, 122–23
SU. *See* Schreiner University
success networks, 122–23
Sun, J. C., 96–97, 98–99, 102, 103
surveys, 32
swatting, 84, 130

tactics, 5–6
taxonomy, 45–46
TBS. *See* turn-based strategy games
Team Liquid, 12
Tespa
　alternative to, 121
　definition of, 130
　governance by, 26–27, 111
third-person shooter games (TPS), 4, 130
threats and intimidation, 97–98
Tiedemann, C., 2, 15
time, 31
The Tipping Point (Gladwell), 38
Title IX, 90–93
Total Tuition and Fees (TTF), 37, 38
tournament structure manipulation, 117, 130
toxic behavior. *See also* harassment
　of homophobia, 86–88
　of misogyny, 86–87, 88–90
　obligation to address, 93–96
　of racism, 86–87, 93
　student-athletes on, 78
　types of, 84–85
TPS. *See* third-person shooter games
training, 12–13
travel expenses, 34
trolling, 130
TTF. *See* Total Tuition and Fees
turn-based strategy games (TBS), 5
Twitch
　definition of, 130
　Overwatch League deal with, 19
　viewers on, 13–14, 15

UCI. *See* University of California at Irvine
uniforms expenses, 34
United States v. Alkhabaz, 102
University of California at Irvine (UCI), 95–96

VACS. *See* Valve Anti-Cheat System
value engineering, 47
Valve Anti-Cheat System (VACS), 117, 130
varsity teams. *See also* intercollegiate varsity sports
　club teams compared to, 43–44
　at SU, 57–59, 60–61
　viewership data, 13–14, 15, 16
Virginia v. Black, 97–98

Wagner, M. G., 2–3, 15
wallhack, 130
Wheeler, Soleil, 88–89
Wilmont, Austin, 88

Xbox, 73–74, 130

YouTube, 13–14, 16

Zimmerman, E., 22–23

Printed in the USA
CPSIA information can be obtained
at www.ICGtesting.com
LVHW012007160324
774517LV00004B/587